Rosie Romances

and Other Rosie the Riveter Stories

Rosie Romances

and Other Rosie the Riveter Stories

*Love stories from World War II
and other stories by women who worked as
Rosies on the home front*

**American
Rosie the Riveter
Association**®

Published in the United States of America by the American Rosie the Riveter Association®, Birmingham, Alabama.

Editor: Nell Carter Branum
Production Assistant: Lucy Case Lewis

The "We Can Do It!" picture on the front cover was painted by graphic artist, J. Howard Miller, as a recruiting poster for Westinghouse Corporation, commissioned by the War Production Coordinating Committee during World War II. It has come to represent all women who worked on the home front during the World War II era. The "We Can STILL Do It!" logo was created by "Rivet" Daniel Branum, using the original artwork. Photos with a notation of "National Archives" are from the World War II photo collection of the National Archives. Photos with a notation of "www.historylink101.com" are from Airforce Image Gallery and can be found at the Planes of World War II Web page.

Copyright © 2008 by the American Rosie the Riveter Association®
Second Printing: August, 2009
ISBN: 978-0-9769260-2-3
Library of Congress Control Number (LCCN): 2008938357

All rights reserved. No part of this work may be reproduced in any form by any means—graphic, electronic, or mechanical—including photocopying, recording, or any process (except for brief quotations in printed interviews or by reviewers, who may quote brief passages to be printed in a newspaper or magazine), without prior written permission of the American Rosie the Riveter Association®. Exception: Each author is granted permission to reproduce her own story and the title page.

Honorary National Headquarters of the American Rosie the Riveter Association® are located at Roosevelt's Little White House Historic Site, Warm Springs, Georgia.

American Rosie the Riveter Association®
www.rosietheriveter.net
(205) 822-4106
fran.carter@juno.com

Copies of this book and other ARRA books may be ordered from:
 ARRA Books
 P. O. Box 188
 Kimberly, AL 35091

Dedication

To all the women who worked during World War II—your steady examples of strength, determination, and patriotism are more vital than ever in the 21st century.

Preface

When the United States entered World War II after the bombing of Pearl Harbor in December 1941, life for Americans changed dramatically. Men and boys who had thought they would join the family business, or work the family farm, or pursue a dream career, suddenly found themselves enlisting or being called up to join the military. Women and girls who had thought they would spend their lives being wives and mothers, perhaps working within a narrow range of traditional careers, suddenly found themselves saying goodbye to husbands, sweethearts, sons, and friends who went away to war. Shortly thereafter, one by one, these women began to roll up their sleeves and tackle the new life that had been thrust upon them. Eventually, more than 6 million women entered the work force in support of the war, and together they are now known as "Rosie the Riveter."

These are the stories of many of those women, presented by the American Rosie the Riveter Association® (ARRA) in this, their fourth and most personal collection of stories yet. These stories are written by the Rosies themselves, or by their descendants, more than 60 years after the end of World War II, and have undergone only minimal editing as necessary for space constraints. Terminology, such as the use of "Air Force" or "Army Air Corps," was left to the discretion of the authors. These stories give a first-hand, coast-to-coast view of life on the home front, as remembered by Rosies who worked in a wide variety of jobs. Hearing their love stories and personal remembrances gives us a window through which to see the reality of those times and how the war affected that part of life closest to their hearts.

Most certainly, the Rosies made an invaluable contribution to the freedom we enjoy today. Most certainly, they opened the world of employment for women. As a "Rosebud" member of ARRA (female descendant of a Rosie), and someone who didn't live through World War II, it is good to see these gifts that are clearly visible as I read these stories. And I discovered some other insights while reading, as well. Here are a few:

First (well, besides the fact that all women of the 1940's

were absolutely beautiful!), these stories point out how mobile the Rosies were. While some had opportunity to work in or near their home towns, many left home and crossed several state lines, often only in their teens, to take jobs in support of the war—a war they had neither asked for nor expected.

There was very little that was easy about the war or about life on the home front. Women had to learn to handle tasks alone, while juggling exhausting schedules, multiple responsibilities, and crushing anxieties and emotions. Yet in story after story, these women—many of them girls, really—considered it a privilege to be a part of that effort. They just did it. They looked for reasons to smile, and they found ways to have fun in spite of it all. With undying patriotism and optimism, they hoped that the war would end and times would be better. But they didn't just hope—they kept on working to make it happen.

Their future was uncertain, and perhaps that helped them to "keep on keeping on." Now we know how the war turned out, but they didn't know it then. Our enemies were determined to conquer the United States, even the world, and they certainly would have succeeded, had it not been for the determination of our troops, our allies, and the matching determination of those on the home front. After the war, the Rosies put that same dogged determination to work as they went back to school, raised children, made marriages work, held down other important jobs, and faced the joys and heartaches that life brought next.

As this book is published, the world is again an uncertain place. These stories give hope and a sense of calm, as we see the example of how these women coped during the war, and after the war, as well. We are still inspired as we see them today, now mostly in their 80's, continuing to make extraordinary contributions. Once again, we need to embrace the strength, dogged determination, patriotism, and optimism of the Rosies.

Thank you, ladies, and may you know that you have given a tremendous gift to the present world, first by accomplishing what you set out to do in the 1940's, then by reminding us, these many years later, that "We can *still* do it!"

Nell Carter Branum
ARRA Book Editor

Contents

1. Strong As a Mule, *Allen* *1*
2. My Life As a Rosie, *Anthoine* *3*
3. I Was a Rosie the Riveter, *Armour* *5*
4. Rosie the Riveter – War Time Memories From 1943 to 1946, *Arundale* *7*
5. Julia's Journey, *Barney/Beckham* *9*
6. Rosie Remembers!, *Baskin* *11*
7. My Rosie the Riveter Story, *Beck* *13*
8. From Farm Girl to Rosie the Riveter, *Beck* *15*
9. How I Met My Husband, *Blume* *17*
10. The "Unauthorized" Army Recruiter, *Blume* *19*
11. Ruby the Riveter, *Bowerman* *21*
12. Born In a Small Town, *Brown* *23*
13. The Love Story of Mike and Julia Bruno, *Bruno* *25*
14. A Rosie's 1945 Christmas, *Carter* *27*
15. John's Side of the Story, *Carter* *29*

16. Love and Hardship Brought Them Together, *Clasen/Pedder* 31

17. For the Duration, *Cole* 33

18. Wartime On the Border, *Cole/Jackson* 35

19. My Romance, *Domenick* 37

20. They Met On the Staten Island Ferry, *Edwards/Smith/Clasen* 39

21. Together We Persevere and Conquer, *Edwards* 41

22. Josey the Riveter, *Feige/Gareis* 43

23. A World War II Romance, *Fiala* 45

24. Oklahoma Sisters to Shipway 7, *Fields* 47

25. How I Met My Husband, *Fields* 49

26. From School Teacher to Rosie the Riveter, *Fisher* 51

27. The War Years, *Flowers* 53

28. Steel-toed Rosie, *Forrester* 55

29. My Rosie Experiences, *Frankel* 57

30. The Post, *Gano/Coulombe* 59

31. How I Remember It, *Gedney* 61

32. My Life Began a Big Change, *Grant* 63

33. The Ones He Left Behind, *Grant/Brummett* 65

34. Hand In Hand, *Grant/Boyes* 67

35. Dear Diary, *Hamilton* 69

36. Rosies Pave the Way for New Careers, *Harrison* 71

37. Reunited in Yosemite, *Hawkins/Peters* 73

38. I Was a Tinker Belle, *Heck* 75

39. Jean's Story—Badge #247, *Holloway* 77

40. Twin Rosies — Double Trouble, *Horton/Taylor* 79

41. High School Sweethearts, *Jayme* 81

42. Our Marriage Was Meant To Be,

   Johnson/Graham/Clasen 83

43. Kentucky Lightnin' Strikes Twice, *Kidd* 85

44. It's Been a Long, Long Time, *Lazerus* 87

45. A World War II Love Story, *Lewis* 89

46. James Was a Blessing In My Life, *Linch/Clasen* 91

47. World War II Experiences, *Mathauser/Rees* 93

48. My Rosie Days, *Mayernick* 95

49. Operating Room Romance, *McCray* 97

50. Rosie the Riveter, *McMillan/Minchew* 99

51. "I Couldn't Jitterbug . . . So I Proposed," *Melillo/Clasen* 101

52. A Love Story, *Miller/Denyer* 103

53. My Trip Out West As a Pioneer of 1944, *Mollberg* 105

54. Another Rosie for World War II, *Moss* 107

55. My War Time Romances, *Myrick* 109

56. My World War II Romance, *Nelsen* 111

57. Moon Over the Palisades, *Nelson* 113

58. Seeing the B-17, Then and Now, *Nickell* 115

59. Forever Young, *Parks* 117

60. Rosie the Riveter, *Pearce* 119

61. My Grandmother Is a Rosie, *Pearce/Minchew* 121

62. Smile—We Did It!, *Penner* 123

63. Fiancé and Father Delay Wedding Four Years, *Pettit/Clasen* 125

64. With Western Union During World War II, *Pope* ... *127*

65. How and Why I Became a Rosie, *Powell* *129*

66. A Wise Mother, *Price* *131*

67. Twins at Boeing, *Rees* *133*

68. My World War II Story, *Roner* *135*

69. A Tale of Women in World War II, *Rowe* *137*

70. The Wartime Wedding of Erma Ellis and Bryce Scudder, *Scudder* *139*

71. Not a Cigarette Between Us, *Sedwick* *141*

72. Rosie the Riveter, *Semrad* *143*

73. And Now...A Word of Appreciation From a Fan, *Asseo* *145*

74. Love Blooms for Doak Aircraft Rosie the Riveter, *Sewell/Hicks* *147*

75. Rosie the Riveter, *Siemens* *149*

76. A World War II Love Story, *Smith* *151*

77. Rosie the Riveter, *Spahn* *153*

78. A Rosie's World War II Travels, *Spriggs* *155*

79. I Want to Marry That Girl, *Tasset* *157*

80. Rosie the Riveter, *Taylor* *159*

81. Courting In the Olden Days, *Thomas* *161*

82. The Behind-the-Heroes Scenes, *Thompson* *163*

83. Our Rosie and Rosebud Story,
    Thompson/Coleman *165*

84. My Second Husband Was My Savior,
    Tinker/Clasen *167*

85. A Commemorative Remembrance, *Treu/Klotz* *169*

86. World War II Home Front Memories, *Tucker* *171*

87. Keeping the Troops Rolling, *Van Alstine* *173*

88. Memorable World War II Occurrences,
    Waldroff *175*

89. My Rosie the Riveter Account, *Walker/Jaynes* *177*

90. My Mother, *Weeks/Grant* *179*

91. Riveting With the Marines, *Whitlock* *181*

92. Wrong Versus Right Brother, *Whitlock* *183*

93. Rosie Works in Arsenal While Waiting For
    the Love of Her Life, *Wills/Wills-Raftery* *185*

94. A Proud Rosie the Riveter, *Wingler* *187*

95. My Mother's Story, *Womack* *189*

96. Where Blue Columbines Grow, *Worthey* *191*

97. Memories of World War II, *Wright* *193*

98. Rosie—The Airplane Mechanic, *Young* *195*

World War II Scrapbook *197*

Index *199*

American Rosie the Riveter Association *205*

During World War II, secretaries, housewives, waitresses, and other women from all over America learned "war work," like these women in the Daytona Beach branch of the Volusia County vocational school.

Strong As a Mule

by Jane E. Allen
Wetumpka, Alabama
about her mother-in-law, Maggie Allen

Maggie, posing on Pet the mule, with her sister, June

    Because most young men in the communities of Troy and Goshen, Alabama, were drafted during World War II, wives and children were left to fend for themselves until these soldiers returned home. Neighbors and friends who owned farms and livestock pitched in to help these families survive during these turbulent years.

    Maggie Allen, my mother-in-law, joined forces with her husband Milton, or "Red" as he was called, to cultivate a huge garden on their farm. Maggie was a hearty country woman who could plow, dig fence posts, and string fence wire alongside her husband. "Strong as a mule," others often remarked.

    During the war years, the two were blessed with crops that produced as much as 1,000 jars of vegetables per sea-son, which they shared with those in need.

Grateful neighbors would often see a weary Maggie riding her mule "Pet" home from a grueling day in the distant fields. A mule was the heart and soul of southern farms during World War II, and was trained to draw the burdensome plows. Maggie loved Pet and rewarded him every day with a treat for his devotion to duty. As she plowed the fields, Maggie often thought about loved ones overseas who were digging foxholes and risking their lives to uphold freedom at home.

In addition, the couple raised large numbers of hogs, chickens, and cows that were later processed and distributed to those families who could not farm.

Although they never sought recognition, Maggie and Red won the County Food Production on the Home Front Award in 1944 for their hard work, enduring spirit, and service to the community.

This remarkable woman was also raising five children and giving birth to another during the war years. The older children cared for the younger ones and were expected to cook the meals, clean the house, do the laundry, and work in the fields – truly a team effort.

After the war, Maggie gave birth to two more children, worked in a sewing factory, and eventually sold insurance. After retirement she would still rise early to go to the fields and pick vegetables, and then freeze and can the bounty for friends and families.

Right up until her death in 1994, Maggie loved telling stories about her experiences during World War II, and she never forgot to give credit to the Lord, her husband and children, and her mule!

Planting Victory Gardens helped win the war!

My Life As a Rosie

by Elizabeth "Betty" Parker Anthoine
Cave Spring, Georgia

"Safely-Dressed" Winners

Safety in dress paid a dividend of a $25 War Bond to Frances Haskell, Engineering Training school, above right, chosen "safest dressed woman war worker" during June. Elizabeth Anthoine, center, ranked second in the contest, and Zell McClellan, left, placed third. Throughout the month of June, Robins Field marked a 67 per cent reduction in lost time accidents, according to Capt. E. R. Proffitt, chief of safety branch.

Newspaper clipping showing how Betty (center) won second place as the "safest dressed woman war worker" for the month of June at Robins Field in the 1940's. First prize was a $25 War Bond.

    I began my career as a Rosie totally by accident. A neighbor asked me to go to Macon with her to apply for a job as a civilian police person. While waiting for her, I was approached and asked if I would like to apply for a defense job and take a test. I agreed.

    The outcome was that my friend failed and I was told to report the next day. Having no transportation, I didn't get to Robins Field until two days later.

    After reporting, taking a physical and more tests, I was sent to my department along with another girl. We found only one other girl in the department who had her training elsewhere, but we were to be trained on the job. Each was assigned to a man on the job.

    We were soon able to rivet, buck rivets, learn the different kinds of rivets, and do whatever else was needed. More and more people came in every few days, and before long we were on our own. I was loaned to other departments a lot, and my least favorite was the engine test. I was glad when the flu epidemic was over in their department.

We were slated for a blackout one night, and someone screwed up. When the warning was given, they turned off the lights, then when the actual blackout was to start, the lights came back on. We were just glad it was a mix-up and not the real thing.

When we needed tools that were not in our tool box, we had to check them out at the tool crib. One day, one of the men came back laughing. He had asked for a bastard file from the lady and she was highly insulted. It was the correct name.

We had a visit from Bob Hope and his entourage, which I didn't attend.

The bathrooms were about a mile apart, and our boss had to load us up, take us, and wait. After a few days, he put me behind the wheel and told me how to change gears (double clutched), then jumped off and left it with me. What fun! Until you tried to double clutch your own car!

When the war ended, we were furloughed for 30 days, then recalled and told to report to our department, or turn in our badge and ID and clear the field. There I was reassigned to aircraft storage where we had a number of B-24's that we repaired, changed protect plugs, turned tires, etc.

My career as a Rosie the Riveter ended in January 1946.

Betty recently enjoyed the azaleas at the Cherry Blossom Festival in Macon, Georgia.

I Was a Rosie the Riveter

by Anna Lee Armour
Wichita, Kansas

Anna and Rodney on their 50th wedding anniversary, standing beside their wedding picture

When World War II started, our country had been going through a Depression. Hundreds of people were without jobs. Wichita had three major aircraft companies: Boeing, Beech, and Cessna. Our government gave them a lot of orders, as we weren't prepared for war at all. People came from all over to work for these plants.

After graduating from high school in 1942, I came to Wichita to attend a National Defense Training School. I believe it was a six-week course. I learned to rivet there.

Since I was only 18, I couldn't get a job at the big plants, as they wouldn't hire anyone under 21. I managed to get a job at Swallow Aircraft Company. They made parts for Beech Aircraft. I think I started out at 45 cents an hour, which was a lot more than I'd ever made before. I was a terrible riveter, so they made me an expediter. I was much better suited for that job.

Up until that time, women didn't wear slacks in public. The men in the plant didn't treat us very nicely at first, as they considered us to be "loose women." After a time, they realized we were just there to do a job and help win the war, and they accepted us.

I was engaged to my husband, Rodney, at that time. He was a mechanic in the Infantry in the 78th Lightning Division. They were stationed at Camp Butner near Durham, North Carolina. He was attending school, however, at Fort Benning near Columbus, Georgia. I quit work to go to Columbus, and we were married there. I went to Durham with him when he completed his schooling. I lived and worked there until I became pregnant with our oldest daughter, Linda. My husband didn't want me to have the baby there, as the Army didn't have very good maternity facilities. I returned home at that time and lived with family during my pregnancy and after our daughter was born.

My husband was then stationed in Germany for one year. He didn't get to see our daughter in person for 15 months. When the war was over, he came back to the States and was discharged from the Army. That was a very happy day.

A lot has happened in our world since then, and there  have been several wars. World War II was the war that the American people believed in, however, and the country did everything it could to help win it. It also really changed the role of women in the United States. They went back to be homemakers after the war, but they knew they had played an important part in the fight for freedom as "Rosie the Riveters."

Rosie the Riveter – War Time Memories From 1943 to 1946

by Hazel Arundale
Oklahoma City, Oklahoma

Arthur and Hazel Arundale in the 1940's

I married my husband, Arthur Arundale, in 1938. We lived in Denver, Colorado. I will never forget where we were on December 7, 1941, when the Japanese bombed Pearl Harbor. It was our anniversary, and we were at home entertaining my husband's parents. The news came over the radio. My husband was working at Fitzsimons Army Hospital in Aurora, Colorado. I was working for Ainsworth and Son in Denver. The war changed all of that.

In 1942, we decided to go to California and work in the aircraft industry. We were both hired at the Douglas El Segundo Plant. Art worked in the Drop Hammer Department. I started as Rosie the Riveter. I worked my way up to the Inspection Department. I had a wonderful boss, "Mr. Snoddy" (his real name).

At that time, I worked with a nice, very quiet, young lady whose name was Norma Jean Baker. When we were new on the job, I asked her what we were supposed to be doing and she replied, "I don't know." I remember her as a very kind, shy, sweet, and beautiful young lady with long dark hair, a great complexion, and a good figure. She was modeling part-time, and she gave me a magazine at work one day. In it she was modeling a blue pant suit. Pant suits were a new fashion then. I wish I had kept the magazine. The next thing I knew, she was Marilyn Monroe.

In 1943, Bob Hope came to our job as the Master of Ceremonies. He gave us pins with the letter "E" for excellence for the work we were doing for the war. Later in 1943, my husband's mother passed away in Denver. We went back for the funeral. Art was called into the Army. I went to work for the Denver Modification Center. We worked on B-17 bombers and other planes. I worked as a Radio Radar Inspector. We had forming boards where we worked up the wiring for the turret retractors and tail gunners. At times we put in 10 hours a day, 7 days a week. We got tired but that was the least we could do for our boys.

We did without many things. Everything was for winning the war. I was a lucky girl because I had a 1941 Chevrolet. You could not buy cars, gas, and food without ration stamps. If you had a pair of silk stockings, you were really lucky. I learned a trick on repairing a run in my silk hose. We wore garter belts in those days, and the tops of my hose were heavier so I could hook the garters on. I would take thread out of the top and put it in a small needle and sew the runs. Once, my sister and I saved gas coupons until we had enough to go see our parents in Oklahoma. The farmers in Oklahoma helped with gasoline on the return trip.

We knew very little about what was going on overseas. They would tell us, "Loose lips sink ships." My husband's letters were checked by the government before I received them. They would have holes in them where things had been cut out that might threaten the soldiers. Sometimes it would be six months before I got a letter and I had no idea where he was. I later found out he was in China, Burma, and India. I did not see him for almost three years. He returned home the latter part of 1946.

When he was discharged, I went to Bakersfield, California, and waited for him. We drove back to Denver. Homes were difficult to find. We got an apartment in the old barracks at Fort Logan. Times were very hard. The job Art had been doing was taken by someone who had been left stateside. He had to start in the laundry and work his way back up. He spent 39 years with the Veterans Administration and retired as Chief of Building Management. We were married almost 60 years when he passed away in 1998. We have two girls, Sharon and Claudia, three grandchildren, and four great-grandchildren. It was a hard life but we made it. I thanked God every day that my husband came home. So many young men did not.

Julia's Journey

by Helen Barney Beckham
Marion, Kansas
about her mother, Julia June Barney

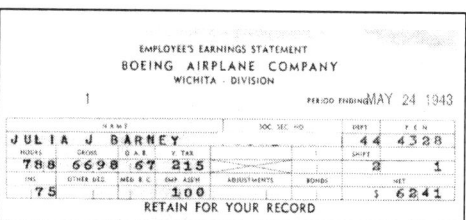

Left: Julia at her desk. This photo appeared in the Boeing Plane Talk newsletter, along with her daughter's photo, as part of an article about the mothers and daughters who worked for Boeing in 1951. Top right: Julia's check stub, showing her earnings (after deductions) of $62.41 for 78.8 work hours. Bottom right: Julia's Boeing badge.

This story is of my mom, Julia J. Barney, who was a "Rosie" during World War II. She was the epitome of all Rosies.

Julia was an energetic, fun-loving person who overcame many of life's obstacles and hardships. She was a very intelligent child of deaf mute parents who taught her to use sign language before she could speak. She loved to sing and dance. Her grandchildren can still sing her favorite song, "How They Gonna Keep Them Down on the Farm?"

Julia was very young when she married my father, W. I. Barney. She thought her role in life would consist of being a wife and mother. However, at the age of 28, after the death of my father, she found herself with little education, three young children, and no Social Security or extensive support groups. She washed dishes at night in a café and enrolled in business courses at El Dorado (Kansas) Junior College.

When WW II began, Julia was one of the first women that worked in the plant area to be hired at Boeing Aircraft Company, Wichita, Kansas. She told us that on the first day at work she saw a man nudge another and say, "What is this world coming to? They've hired a woman, and a half pint at that!"

Julia rose to the position of Clerk Supervisor in Tool Engineering. During this time, she and the second shift worker that held the same position kept a journal as a way to record daily job-related activities. Often they added their thoughts on the war and its effect on their personal lives. These journals are now in the Archives at Wichita State University. They were transcribed by Dr. Judith Johnson, Professor, who has endowed the University with her project entitled *Women During Wartime*.

Mother worked 10-12 hours a day, 7 days a week, and was commuting on a Boeing bus, 70 miles round trip. We moved to Planeview, a housing project for Boeing workers, when a unit became available.

I was amazed how the Boeing workers helped each other. When she needed gas for our car to visit our grandmother, the employees shared their gas ration stamps. I remember seeing them put a "newer" tire on our car to replace a worn one.

After the war, Mother worked for the Reconstruction Finance Company at Boeing. We were raised by an absentee, single, working mom, who was very successful at both jobs.

The 1,000th B-29 made at Boeing, Wichita, 1945. No doubt there are many Rosies in this photo!

Rosie Remembers!

by Minnie Furn Baskin
Sun City, Arizona

Furn in the 1940's

    I was born in Harmony, Arkansas, seven miles from Clarksville. I graduated in the 1940-41 year. My first job was in high school as a time-keeper for an auto mechanics shop. From there, I worked in a laundry.

    Then I went to Little Rock and worked for Arkansas Ordnance Plant (Ford, Bacon & Davis), as a "powder scooper," making anti-aircraft shells. I worked there until the girl next to me had an explosion, knocking her back against the wall. Her glasses saved her eyes, but she was covered with splinters and was taken to the hospital. After that I went home, but I came to Phoenix later that year. It took three days getting here, as we kept being side-tracked for troop trains. I got here on a Thursday, went to Goodyear on Friday, and went to work on Monday as "Rosie the Riveter." My partner and I were chosen to check and replace any bad rivets, so we worked in tight places at times.

My boyfriend, T-Sgt. David K. Baskin, was stationed in Muroc, California. He came by here on his way to Washington, D. C. for a special assignment. We were married on September 8, 1945, while he was here.

He was to go overseas, but this assignment gave him enough points to be discharged. He got back to Phoenix on December 24, 1945. I became a housewife and he worked at Arizona Hardware for a few months. Then he worked at Reynold's Metal Company for 27 years, missing only 5 days. He passed away on December 29, 1990.

I moved to Sun City in 2005, and am so blessed to have a son, a daughter, and three grandchildren living in the Phoenix and Glendale area. I'll always be proud to have been a part of the "We can do it" gang.

Furn in 2007

My Rosie the Riveter Story

by Genevieve E. Beck
Douglasville, Georgia

Genevieve, looking festive in 2003

My name is Genevieve E. Beck. I was a "Rosie" during World War II. In February 1943, my Daddy was working for a machinery plant in Orlando, Florida, making parts for planes and ships, doing his part to help the war. Daddy said, "Go and work for your country." I had been married since 1936 to Woodrow Wilson Beck, and in 1940 we had a baby girl, named Bea; but the marriage didn't work out, so Bea and I were living back home with my parents. I signed up to be a sheet metal mechanic, and was sent to Nashville, Tennessee for six weeks of training.

After training, I came home to Florida and to the Orlando Air Base for repairing large bombers, the B-27 and many others. As "Rosie the Riveter," my work on the planes was as follows: The bombers had been shot up in the war zones, making holes in the planes. Working with a partner, we would measure and cut the metal and repair the plane. My partner and I would swap off on the job, as we both knew how to drive and buck the rivet.

With four or more people working on the same plane, we all were required to go up in the plane while it was being tested, to see if we had done a good job. I had never been flying before and I was afraid I would be sick, so I was told to check out a bucket from the tool department.

We worked 10 to 12 hours a day. I would go at night to visit the USO and talk to the service men and women.

There I met a paratrooper. He was a very good dancer and so was I; we did a lot of dancing and we would also go to the skating rink. We both had our own skates, so he taught me to dance on my skates; what fun it was! We dated about six months before he was shipped out and our paths went different ways.

My father and I both had Saturday and Sunday off. We would travel home to our family in Titusville, Florida. My daughter, Bea, was three years old; we had a good time together. Daddy and I both worked hard and long hours, but we didn't mind, for we were helping our country.

While I was being "Rosie" over at the Orlando Air Base, the government wanted to guard the beaches at Titusville, my home town. The service men needed a place to stay, so my father offered the upstairs of our home. These boys, serving in the Army, Coast Guard, and Navy, would rotate from time to time; it was great to meet all the men. They stayed with us until the war was over. I was happy to be a member of the Everritt family, doing their part for the war.

Sammy Laughlin Beck (left), age 19, and her sister, Clara Laughlin Shuits, age 18, on their way to work one day in 1944

From Farm Girl to Rosie the Riveter

by
Sammy Laughlin Beck

Oklahoma City, Oklahoma

On December 7, 1941, the Japanese bombed Pearl Harbor and the U. S. was at war. The young men either volunteered or were drafted into military service, including my two older brothers. Homes had a blue star in the window for each military person, and a gold star if the person lost their life. We had two blue stars in our window, as my two older brothers enlisted.

We used ration stamps to get food and we grew a large victory garden. There was a scrap iron drive. We gathered nuts, bolts, and any small pieces of iron we could find, and walked down a path and across a field to meet the rural mail carrier with buckets filled with scrap iron. The postman weighed the scrap iron and paid us a few cents per pound.

My friend Leona was in Oklahoma City and she asked me to join her and find a job, so I left the farm in Pontotoc County, Oklahoma and came to the big city. On arrival, I found that she and her sister Gertrude lived in a one-room basement apartment with one full-size bed. Gertrude was not thrilled with the cramped sleeping arrangement, so I wrote my sister Clara, age 18, and asked her to join me. On the day she arrived, I met her at the bus station and we found an apartment and moved in the same day. We went to the employment office and got a job at the Douglas Aircraft Plant in Midwest City, Oklahoma, making 67 cents per hour. We soon received a 5 cent per hour raise.

At Douglas, my partner and I applied the aluminum skin to the center wing section of the C-47 cargo plane. The aluminum skin section was put in place and rivets were placed in holes and covered with masking tape. My partner crawled inside the wing to buck the rivets as I shot them in with an air gun.

My sister Clara was a drill press operator and we worked the swing shift. One evening as we walked along the sidewalk near our apartment, two young sailors whistled at us. We slowed our pace so they could catch up. The four of us were good friends, and we kept in touch while Charlie and Lee Roy served their country in the South Pacific.

Women wore pants or coveralls and steel-toed shoes to work at Douglas. Before WW II, a woman's place was in the home. Now they were wearing whatever they chose and finding work outside the home in droves. Nylon was developed for use in parachutes, and women had nylon stockings. The world was never the same.

When the picture on the previous page was taken, my sister Clara and I were on our way to the bus stop to catch a bus to work at Douglas Aircraft Plant. We are both wearing our badges. The picture was made in a little booth with a camera. You dropped in a coin and posed and your photo popped out of a slot. This was our first job. We were straight off the farm and had never been so far from home. It was approximately 95 miles from our farm to Midwest City, Oklahoma, which is a suburb of Oklahoma City.

In 1945, the U. S. dropped the atomic bomb on Japan, and a ceremonial surrender took place on the deck of the battleship USS *Missouri* on September 2, 1945. This was when the Japanese admitted defeat and surrendered to America. Shortly thereafter, the defense jobs were terminated. Lee Roy and Charlie came home, and after a courtship, we had a double wedding at Wayne, Oklahoma.

How I Met My Husband

by Odean Gregg Blume
Aurora, Colorado

Odean and Alton Blume in 1939

In August 1939, I was working as a waitress at the officers' club in Fort Brown at Brownsville, Texas. My salary was $21.00 a month. I worked eight hours, five days a week, and my hourly pay was about 13 cents, no tips. On Saturday, I was given a fresh-baked pie to take home.

On Saturday, August 28, I went to pick up my pie. I didn't realize that two soldiers were watching until I went inside. The manager's phone was ringing and it was one of the soldiers that was watching me, Alton Blume. He asked the manager who I was, and asked if he could speak to me. I talked with him a few minutes and he invited me to a rodeo. I told him that I would have to get permission from my brother-in-law. I told him who my brother-in-law was and where he worked. Fort Brown was a small post, so everyone knew each other. My brother-in-law said that Alton was a good guy and it was all right for me to go with him.

Alton told his friend when they were watching me, "I am going to marry that girl." It must have been love at first sight for him.

We had three weeks before he was to leave Fort Brown to play war games all the way to Fort Bliss at El Paso, Texas. We spent those weeks going to rodeos, to the beach, and sitting on the front porch talking.

On September 28, the soldiers marched out of Fort Brown for their journey of war games. It was a beautiful parade—the soldiers sitting straight with chins up, horses shiny clean, and highly polished saddles. The streets of Brownsville were lined with people to cheer the soldiers on their way.

The first of December, my sister and I went to El Paso. We shared a house with another military family, four miles from Fort Bliss. After playing war games all day, Alton would walk the four miles to visit me. We were married December 20, 1939 in the El Paso courthouse by a Judge, with Alton's First Sergeant and his wife as witnesses. We couldn't have a wedding, because soldiers below the rank of Sergeant were not allowed to be married. The Sergeant was a true friend and never revealed our secret.

During the war, I worked as an Army recruiter. We didn't have a honeymoon until the war was over. Christmas of 1945, Alton had 30 days furlough and we traveled by bus to Alabama, Texas, and back to Denver, Colorado, where he would be stationed at Lowery Air Force Base. We had 52 years together. He died May 27, 1991, on Memorial Day. He was buried at Fort Logan National Cemetery in Littleton, Colorado, with Honors.

Odean and Alton in 1985

The "Unauthorized" Army Recruiter

by
Odean Gregg Blume

Aurora, Colorado

Odean Blume, Army recruiter, 1941-1943

In the early 1940's, the Army transferred my husband, Alton, to recruiting service in Oklahoma City, Oklahoma. He later opened a recruiting office at a substation located in Altus (in southwest Oklahoma). I volunteered to help Alton and his part-time secretary by typing records and filing. I also traveled with Alton as we put up those famous posters of Uncle Sam pointing his finger and exclaiming, "I Want You." We placed the posters in store windows and on utility poles all over southwest Oklahoma.

Every few weeks, Alton had to report his activities in person at the recruiting headquarters in Oklahoma City. One week while Alton was away, six young men came into the office and wanted to enlist. They were very anxious and didn't want to wait until Alton returned. Linda, the secretary, asked me what we could do.

We knew how to process them, but were not authorized recruiters. Nevertheless, we completed the paperwork according to proper procedure and enlisted them into the

Army. We then escorted the young men to the bus station and put them on the bus for Oklahoma City.

When they arrived at headquarters, the commander asked Alton how they could have been processed with no authorized recruiter on duty in Altus. Of course, Alton didn't have an answer, but suspected that I had enlisted them. He also knew that he was in trouble. At the time, no service men lower than the rank of Sergeant were allowed to be married. The following morning, the commander made a surprise visit to the recruiting station in Altus and wanted an explanation as to how those young men had been enlisted. I wasn't in the office on that particular day, but Alton had to confess that he was married and that I had enlisted the men. The commander said he wanted to meet "that spunky young lady." Alton came home for lunch and told me the commander would be in our apartment that evening for dinner.

When the commander arrived, he told us that Alton could be court-marshaled and discharged from the Army for being married . . . not to mention the fact that six young men had been enlisted without an authorized recruiter in the office. But the commander also knew that my husband was a good soldier and recruiter. Instead of discharging him, he gave us permission to be married and promoted Alton to the rank of Sergeant. Needless to say, we were relieved.

Odean with her cute Yorkie companion, Beau Jo, in 2004

After the attack on Pearl Harbor, all of the substations were closed and the induction center was opened in Tulsa. The commander felt that I was a good recruiter and enlisted me into special services. I worked at the induction center from 1941 to 1943. Yes, they actually put me to work doing the same job that had almost caused my husband to be discharged from the Army!

Ruby the Riveter

by Ruby Lee Eversole Bowerman
Mount Airy, Maryland

Ruby Bowerman in the 1940's (left) and more recently

My name is Ruby Bowerman, and I was born Ruby Lee Eversole in Rowe, Oklahoma, on March 26, 1919. I grew up in Oklahoma. When I was 23, shortly after the attack on Pearl Harbor, I was working at Safeway and was seriously considering joining the WAVES (Women Accepted for Voluntary Emergency Service). Around that same time, two of my friends were heading out to California to see about getting jobs at the Lockheed plant in the Los Angeles area.

I decided to go ahead and accompany my friends to Los Angeles, thinking that I would take a look before making my final decision. We didn't waste any time in getting on with it. The very next day, my two friends and I found ourselves on an overcrowded train, headed for Los Angeles. We had to stand up for a good part of the trip because the train was so overpacked with soldiers, who were also heading out to Los Angeles to ship out to the Pacific Theater. The train trip turned out to be quite a memorable experience, and we talked and sang with the service men for most of the way.

When we arrived in Los Angeles, we found housing right away, and put in our applications at Lockheed. We started work the very next day. What an experience! I started out as a riveter on the aileron of the Lockheed P-38 Lightning, and continued in that position until the end of the war. I was proud to learn that it was a squadron of these very planes that would shoot down the plane carrying Admiral Yamamoto, the Japanese leader who had planned the attack on Pearl Harbor. I was but one woman, but felt very much a part of our country's committed effort.

Within my group of roommates, as was common in those days, none of us owned a car. The street cars were the usual mode of getting around, and we adjusted quickly to taking them wherever we needed to go. We all joined the graveyard shift at Lockheed. Many nights would find us at the Hollywood Palladium, a big dance hall, where we would dance through the night, often leaving just enough time to get home for a change of clothes before heading back out to work. There was always the call for blood donations, and many times, my friends and I would all go together to the local blood bank to do our part. This was usually on the way home from work in the morning.

The war was a difficult time in our country, but I loved what I did during those times. It was a time when it was important for everyone to pitch in, and my friends and I did our best for Lockheed and those P-38's. I loved serving my country in the best way that I could.

Near the end of the war, I went to a dance for tall-statured people called "The Tip-Toppers," and it was there that I met Jack Bowerman. Jack was 6 feet tall, and I was 5 feet 9 inches. Three months after we met, Jack and I were married. We have enjoyed a wonderful 61 years together, have raised three great children, and have seven grandchildren. I have worked extensively in nursery schools and have had the opportunity to work with many, many children over the years. This has been work that I have loved dearly. Jack and I have had the opportunity to travel together to many places in the world, and have enjoyed many wonderful adventures together on our trips. God has blessed us so much, and we are proud to be Americans.

Born In a Small Town
by Leola Marie Womack Brown
Mayfield, Kentucky

Leola Marie Brown in the 1940's

My name is Leola Marie Womack Brown, and this story describes my life during the war. I was born in the small town of Mayfield, Kentucky. I was a daughter, a sister, a wife, and a mother. At age 20, I went to work at the Viola Naval Ordnance Plant in Viola, Graves County, Kentucky.

I was married to Bill Brown, who went into the Army in 1943. I lived with my mother in Mayfield, Kentucky during this difficult time. Every evening I wrote letters to my husband, and often to my brother, who was also serving in the Army. I took care of my baby sister and infant nephew while my mother and sister-in-law worked shifts at the Viola ammunition factory.

At the plant, I worked in a small room, wore coveralls,

and sat at a table with eight women. Wooden trays were brought in, and my job was to push a felt-like material into tiny brass vial-like containers, using a tool like a crochet hook. When I finished the 100-200 vials in each tray, I passed the vials along for tetrol to be added. Supervisors oversaw the work.

One day, government workers visited the facility. Being young, with minimal work experience, I was so nervous about their presence that I dropped an entire tray. I was horrified. All work was stopped immediately and did not resume until every single vial was accounted for. We had been told to always be very careful and never to crimp the vials incorrectly, or the whole plant would blow up. The only exit from the room I worked in was through a larger room that contained explosives, so if there was an explosion there was no way out. Fortunately, my mishap did not end in disaster.

My baby, Dave, was a few months old when I went to work, and I worked for about a year. Dave developed pneumonia, and I stopped working to take care of him. At that time, there were no wonder drugs to treat pneumonia. Medical care in my town was minimal, with almost all the doctors away at war. In fact, my son was breech, and while I was giving birth in 1944, the doctor gave up on me and my baby and left the room, leaving us to die. My mother got the nurse and begged her to finish the delivery. We both survived, and my son was born healthy, but with a broken shoulder.

At the end of the war, my husband and brother returned home unharmed, and small town life took on a more normal pace. I had more children and more work experiences, and close family to share it all with.

The Love Story of Mike and Julia Bruno

by Julia Regina Bruno
Brooklyn, New York

Mike and Julia Bruno on their wedding day in November 1945 (left) and on their 54th anniversary in 1999

My husband and I met while I was working in a linen factory on the first floor of a building that houses the famous Katz Delicatessen in Lower Manhattan, New York. Some fellows came in and said they were opening a Social Club on the top floor, and invited us to come. This fellow named Mike was an artist, and he made the signs and decorations for the club. On Opening Night, Mike and another fellow walked me home. By the time we reached home, Mike asked me for a date to go to the Paramount Theatre to see Frank Sinatra, and I accepted. Since I was not allowed to date at that time (I had 10 brothers who made sure of that!), I told my parents that a girlfriend wanted me to come over to wash her hair and put curlers in it, and instead I met Mike.

When Pearl Harbor happened in 1941, Mike and I were in a theater watching a Clark Gable movie. They interrupted the movie to tell everyone about the attack. That day, on the way home, Mike said he was going to enlist in the Army, which he did. In the Army, Mike was the one who painted all those cartoon-like figures and names on the sides of the fighter planes.

During the war, I worked as a welder at two different shipyards, one in Kearney, New Jersey, and the other in Port Newark. My girlfriends and I all lived on the Lower East Side in New York City. I had been doing defense work for an airplane company named American Rolbal in downtown Brooklyn. I worked on the drill press, making airplane parts. We were not comfortable working there, because, believe it or not, during wartime, the regular workers at this defense plant went on strike! We were offered welding work on the ships in New Jersey. There were six of us, and someone would drive us there every day in a car and pick us up at night. We each paid 25 cents a day to the driver. These were very fulfilling jobs because we were helping our country.

While Mike was in the Army, I started to date a fellow named Victor. One night while having dinner at my house, Victor's sister came and called up to us from the street (we lived on the first floor) that Victor was drafted and had to report to a certain ship immediately. We wrote many letters and were getting pretty serious. But I never really forgot about Mike, and apparently he never really forgot about me. He was medically discharged after serving for almost four years. At the end of the war, Mike came to where I was organizing a victory block party, and we went to many victory parties together. Then I had to write a Dear John letter to Victor, because in November 1945, Mike and I were married. Now we have been married for almost 63 years! Mike became a designer in the garment industry. We have lived in Gerritsen Beach, Brooklyn, for 50 years. We live for our children, grandchildren, and great-grandchildren. They give us much joy.

Julia and some of her "Rosie" girlfriends at a Coney Island photo booth on their day off. Julia is the front seat passenger.

I am a member of the American Rosie the Riveter Association, and my name is listed in the National World War II Memorial in Washington, D.C. It wasn't all easy, but we would do it all over again. We are proud to be American and to have been a part of the work force and the Army during WW II.

A Rosie's 1945 Christmas

by Dr. Frances Tunnell Carter
Birmingham, Alabama

Fran in 1943, when she worked as a riveter and wore her special paratrooper's wings and fraternity key

I had left my job as a teacher in rural Mississippi in the spring of 1943 to work as a riveter on B-29's at Bechtel McComb Parsons aircraft modification plant in Birmingham, Alabama. It was challenging but enjoyable work, but after a while, they wanted to transfer me to a plant in Florida. My parents back in Mississippi said "No," and although I was 21, I still felt constrained to obey them.

There were two ways to get released from the job: being pregnant or taking a job teaching. Being single, I chose the latter and went back to Mississippi for another year of teaching. Then I enrolled at the University of Southern Mississippi in Hattiesburg to complete college.

Hattiesburg is near Camp Shelby, a large military installation. I began working at the USO, entertaining the troops. One rule was, "Never leave the premises with a soldier. He might be somebody's husband!"

During all this time, I was falling in love with a special paratrooper named John, who was serving in Europe. We weren't engaged when he went overseas, but we could both shoot a pretty good line through the V-mail. Mail had trouble reaching him part of the time, but somewhere along the line we started planning to get married. I don't know when he exactly asked me; he says he didn't have to. He sent some money to a jeweler in Hattiesburg and I went down and picked out my engagement ring. Not very romantic, but in those days you settled for what you could get!

At last the war was over, and John arrived back in the States. He was coming on a troop train from New York to be mustered out in Camp Shelby! It was during the Christmas holidays, but I stayed over in the dorm to wait. When he got there, he called me about midnight and asked me to meet him at the Hattiesburg bus station.

I beat it down there as fast as I could, and that bus station was nothing but wall-to-wall soldiers. I could hardly shove through them. I bet I could have gotten a hundred dates that night!

We were afraid we might not recognize each other; he had been gone so long. But we needn't have worried. Suddenly, we were together and oblivious to everyone else. We've been together ever since, happily working on "the rest of the story."

Fran and John speak often to school and community groups. Fran dresses as she did while a Rosie, and John wears his original paratrooper uniform. At this gathering in 2007, they shared with school library media specialists, 62 years after that 1945 Christmas.

John's Side of the Story

by Dr. John T. Carter
about his wife, Frances Tunnell Carter
Birmingham, Alabama

Left: Fran and John on a visit while she was working in Birmingham. Right: Fran with her niece, Ann, reading a letter from John while he was overseas.

This story is about Frances Tunnell Carter, a Rosie.

It didn't occur to me that I'd fall in love with Fran. I had seen her only a couple of times on visits to the junior college in Mathiston, Mississippi, where she was earning her entire way through. (She had arrived on campus with 38 cents and the promise of a job.) I also met J.W., her clearly possessive boyfriend. I couldn't blame him., but to me, she was just a very pleasant diversion.

Our trails crossed again the next summer in the small college town where I was working and she had enrolled in summer courses to qualify for a defense certificate to teach school. This was in 1942, just after Pearl Harbor. She said J.W. was in the Navy. We saw each other three or four times that summer, and once, she referred to "a John I used to know." I perked up. That must have meant that she and J.W., whose name was really John, had broken up, and now the coast was clear. By the time she left for her teaching assignment, I was head over heels in love.

She invited me to come to see her one weekend on the small farm where her family lived near Pontotoc, Mississippi. I hitch-hiked to Pontotoc, and when I asked a taxi driver if he knew where the Tunnell farm was, he said, "Sure. I took a sailor out there last week!" That really knocked the wind out of my sails! When I asked Fran if that sailor was J.W. she said, "Yes." Turns out they had not broken up; the "John she used to know" was *another* John, who had preceded J.W. He was in the Army Air Corps. I saw that if I rated at all, I'd be the third-string John on her list! I resolved to work my way up to first.

In April 1943, I was called to active duty in the Army. Fran went to Birmingham, Alabama, to work in an airplane factory. I saw her only about three times before I joined the paratroops and was sent overseas to Europe. I still wasn't sure of my status among the "three Johns." I figured I could shoot a better line through the V-mail than either of them; but due to the battle situations, my mail sometimes had a hard time finding me. We had started planning our life together, but she was too tender-hearted to tell J.W. while he was in a hell-hole in the Pacific.

Once she wrote that J.W. was on his way home. I knew he'd have marrying on his mind, and I honestly wasn't sure what Fran's next letter would say. It took it three weeks to come, but it was worth waiting for. She had told J.W. she couldn't marry him and had kissed him goodbye (I suppose). Now we were free to make real plans, rather than just dream. I got home in December 1945, we were married in March, and the dreams have been coming true ever since.

John and Fran demonstrate a "WW II two-step" at a speaking engagement in 2006

Love and Hardship Brought Them Together

by Jonnie Melillo Clasen, Donna Clasen Pedder, Douglas "Michael" Clasen, and Darcy Clasen about their mother and mother-in-law, Laura Belle Seim Clasen

Left: Laura and James, visiting a Minnesota lake in July 1930, shortly before their wedding. Right: Laura with her daughter, Donna, around the time they moved to Riverside, California.

Laura Belle Seim had no idea she would wind up living in southern California and working in support of WW II when she married James Eugene Clasen in September 1930 in Minneapolis, Minnesota. Laura was the more outgoing half of the couple. Her love of learning, art, music, and dance reflected the Swedish heritage of her mother, Matilda "Tilda" Forslund. But it was also Tilda's unhappy marriage that caused Laura to leave her Minneapolis home at age 15 before finishing high school. Laura met James in between working as a "live-in mother's helper" in the 1920's, and moving briefly to Chicago to live with her Aunt Mame and work as a newspaper proofreader.

"I think Mom may have been really disappointed when she and Dad didn't go to a nice resort for their honeymoon," says

Laura's youngest son, Michael. "Apparently, part of their honeymoon was spent roughing it in this cabin on a lake where Dad took her fishing."

There was a quiet strength in James' reserved personality that probably attracted the teen-aged Laura to her future husband. Born in 1905, James was seven years older than Laura. James had been forced into adulthood at age 12 after his mother, Florence Elizabeth, took his two younger brothers and moved to a new life in California, leaving him behind to work the family farm with his father, Peter, in Maple Plain.

The Clasen women had adventurous spirits. James' maternal grandmother, Mary Lou Maddox, and her sister were mail-order brides "brought over from England" to marry James' grandfather and great uncle. That adventurous spirit rubbed off on Laura. She convinced James to take an offer from his mother, Florence, to move the family, which then included two children, to California and live with her. Laura had been cooking and cleaning without indoor plumbing at the Maple Plain farm, where they had moved to help Grandpa Peter.

"In 1937, Dad drove Mom, my little brother Darcy, and me to Riverside in a square car with a huge box of our belongings tied to the back end," explains Laura's daughter, Donna Clasen Pedder, who was then 6 years old. "Dad went to work at the Long Beach shipyards. We had a Victory Garden in the backyard, and there was an avocado tree and an orange tree," says Donna, adding that Laura worked for a year in a war-related job. "I remember listening to war news from London on a radio that was on top of the refrigerator in the kitchen."

In the 1960's, Laura took a high-school equivalency test and entered college while her son, Michael, was in high school. She went on to get a master's degree and retire from a career as a high school English teacher. Her oldest son, Darcy, became a highly-decorated Marine Corps Lieutenant Colonel during the 1960's, with 800 combat missions in Vietnam.

Following her husband's death, Laura began writing short stories, moved to Reno where her son Michael lived, and started ballroom dancing and painting. She died just after her 85th birthday.

For the Duration
by
Shirley Marie
Jackson Cole

Winchester, Tennessee

Shirley in her Vultee uniform in 1943 (left), and with her husband, Cecil, in 2005

In January 1943, I left Chrysler Corporation in Michigan to work at Vultee Aircraft in Nashville, Tennessee, "for the duration." As part of the hiring agreement, I purchased a toolbox and wrenches, center punch, ball peen hammer, and several types of pliers and screwdrivers. We rotated jobs, many of which were physically demanding and made us ill.

For six months, I worked the graveyard shift, installing fuel bags on the inner wings of airplanes, until my eyes swelled shut. Then I re-worked an inner wing not passing inspection. Outside the jig, I held bolts while the other employee worked inside the job to remove taps, communicating by tapping. Each rework took about an hour and a half. Later, I rotated to the paint booth and wore plastic gloves until I had a skin reaction and transferred to installing armor plate and the relief system, and served as first aid squad warden on my shift.

Another rotation involved removing a defective part inside the airplane suspended from the ceiling. Climbing a ladder into the cockpit, we carried electric drills. One day when my coworker crawled into the cockpit to use a 220 volt drill, something went wrong and she screamed, "I'm slowly being electrocuted!" I used my first aid training to help her.

On another rotation, one person was inside the plane's tail and another was outside, straddling the fuselage. Working outdoors in the summertime in the South, the metal was so hot it burned us. No air inside the plane made the heat suffocating. So we rotated tasks, until I got heat exhaustion and missed a week's work. I did this job until my next rotation to the final assembly stock room. I went throughout the plant on a special badge, locating engineers and parts, getting work orders for changes, going to the supply room, and collecting new parts to keep assembly people going. At one point, I issued parts to deaf workers in an area where they riveted.

At Christmas, servicemen stayed in our home. At the YWCA's Industrial Girls' Club, I served as vice-president and president, and attended camp in Henderson, North Carolina, where female industrial workers from several southern states met. I went with the Central Church of Christ chorus to visit patients and sing at Thayer Military Hospital on White Bridge Road. I participated in YWCA and USO activities. At their dances, music came from a jukebox in the gym, and refreshments were served in the cafeteria. We served refreshments, and sat and talked with servicemen, while others danced. Periodically, we were asked to circulate, speaking to everyone, especially if the servicemen were shy.

After the war, my brother was in Nashville's Thayer V. A. Hospital on White Bridge Road, where I met my husband-to-be. He was in the bed next to my brother.

Wartime On the Border

by Cheryl Ann Cole
Winchester, Tennessee
about her mother, Shirley Marie Jackson Cole
and her grandmother, Clara Louise Owens Jackson

Mother and daughter Rosies, Clara Louise Jackson (left) and Shirley Marie Cole, in the early 1950's

In the late 1930's and early 1940's, my maternal grandparents and mother lived at Port Huron, Michigan, on the Canada-U. S. border. Long before the U. S. was involved in WW II, they felt the effects of the war in Europe, because Canada, as a member of the British Commonwealth, was at war, and life had already changed for those entering and leaving the two countries. Friends and family in Canada had served in WW II and returned before the U. S. even entered the war.

After Pearl Harbor, things changed even more dramatically. The Blue Water International Bridge connected the twin cities of Port Huron, Michigan and Sarnia, Ontario, across the mouth of the St. Clair River where it emptied into Lake Huron. This waterway was part of the system linking the Great Lakes to the Saint Lawrence Seaway and the ocean. Ocean-going vessels frequented the river, bringing goods back and forth from Detroit, up the river and into the lake system. As a result, it was important to secure the area. The Coast Guard heavily patrolled the area to ensure that no airplanes flew under the bridge, and watched for seaplanes attempting to blow up the bridge. Security on both sides of the border tightened.

On the U. S. side, my grandparents were appointed air raid wardens for a designated segment of the countryside. There were frequent air raid warnings and drills. When the air raid siren was heard, all activity immediately stopped. Window shades were pulled down, and lights extinguished. Not even a flashlight or a candle could be left burning. Steps were taken to ensure that no lights burned and the countryside was in complete darkness. Outside fires were extinguished.

Shirley in 2003, holding a book that she co-authored with her daughter, Cheryl. The book, entitled Little Wicker Basket, *is a collection of stories about the history of Shirley's church in Michigan. It was published for the church's 75th anniversary.*

My grandmother drove a circuit to make sure no lights burned anywhere in the district. Her entire family helped. My mother drove the car with no lights burning. My grandparents rode, looking and checking diligently to make sure no lights were burning in the countryside. Sometimes they were asked to go to special locations to make other checks.

My Romance

by Mary Lou FitzGerald Domenick
Jeannette, Pennsylvania

Mary Lou and Pat were married for 41 years. During the war, Mary Lou worked as a draftsman, making engineering drawings for ingot molds in steel production.

It was a happy time. The war was over and all the boys were coming home. There were parties and dances everywhere. In the towns across western Pennsylvania, the Volunteer Fire Company has a building to hold the shiny red fire truck. Next door is the Social Hall. Every Friday and Saturday night there was a band for dancing. Most towns also had an American Legion Post with a large, polished dance floor. The men who fought the battles in World War I welcomed the returning "GI's" with open arms and a card that got them into American Legion activities. The weekend always brought a good dance band.

Then there were the big night clubs: William Penn Tavern in Greensburg, Twin Coaches and Vogue Terrace in McKeesport, and the Holiday House in Monroeville. They booked professional entertainment that included the "Big Bands" of Tommy Dorsey, Benny Goodman, Sammy Kaye, Kay Kyser, and Vaughn Monroe. These clubs held hundreds of people. Couples sat around small tables. As the crowd grew, more tables were added until you could not move on the dance floor.

The highlight of the evening was when a girl came to your table to take the souvenir picture. It showed a happy group – boys in new suits, girls in pretty party dresses with flowers in their hair.

There was one more place, The Pavilion, a festive summer building with a roof and dance floor, with open sides to make for cooler dancing under the summer sky. Fate brought me and the man I fell in love with, to meet at a C.Y.O. (Catholic Youth Organization) dance at the Oakford Park Pavilion. My Pat graduated from school and entered the Navy Submarine Service aboard the USS *Cabezon* (SS 334). Pearl Harbor was his home base. He cruised all over the Pacific from Antarctica to Alaska. While in Alaska, the Captain and crew earned a medal for outstanding service. They submerged under the polar ice to chart waters, some places only inches above and below the submarine, thus helping the nuclear submarine USS *Nautilus*, in a later time, make its famous trip from the Pacific to the Atlantic under the polar ice. He was discharged and left immediately for Wake Forest College in Wake Forest, North Carolina.

I had come to the dance with a girlfriend. We were waiting for the music to start when Helen said, "There is Junior Domenick. He is just home from the Navy." I looked across the dance floor and saw a tall, dark-haired, handsome young man talking with a group of girls. He came over to talk to Helen. She introduced him to me and he asked me to dance. We danced together several times and he drove Helen and me home. He called for dates and we started going steady. We got engaged Christmas Eve, and were married the following year on March 31, 1951. We have two sons: Robert Patrick Domenick, Esq., an attorney with his own private practice; and Jeffrey J. Domenick, Managing Editor of *Valley News Dispatch*, a Pittsburgh area paper. Our little girl, Mary Caitlyn, we lost as an infant.

We were together for 41 years. I had a happy marriage. Pat opened the world to me. Being a Construction Engineer, he worked across the country from the Atlantic to the Pacific and to the south, to Birmingham, Alabama and New Orleans. Whether we were at a historical site, theater, concert, or sitting quietly at home, he made it fun. I like to think he enjoyed it, too. He would say, "When you are married to an Irish girl, you never have two days alike." Then he would laugh.

They Met On the Staten Island Ferry

by
Jonnie Melillo Clasen
and Paul Edwards
Columbus, Georgia

about Paul's mother,
Dorothy Garzik Edwards
and his sister,
Dorothy "Dottie"
Edwards Smith

Dorothy Edwards and her daughter, Mary Ann, saying goodbye to Paul in the 1940's at Sacred Heart Academy, a private school in Sharon, Massachusetts, that Paul attended.

Dorothy Garzik was a dancer in New York City burlesque shows starring Mae West in the early 1900's, when she met Walter J. Edwards on the Staten Island Ferry crossing the Hudson River. "My godfather, Uncle Joe Grady, was the captain of the ferry they met on," says Paul Edwards, Dorothy's youngest son. "When she got married, she was in show business. She was very pretty."

Dorothy, born in 1905, was from Bayonne, New Jersey. Walter, a descendant of Irish immigrants, was born in New York City's "Hell's Kitchen" in 1902. Dorothy died in 1980, more than a decade after Walter's death in 1963.

"They actually ran away from home to get married," says Paul. "Times were very bad back then, and I know they didn't go on a honeymoon, because they lived in a cold-water flat after they were married.

"They settled down in Long Island, and that's where it all started. My father joined the Army right after they got married, and was stationed at Picatinny Arsenal in New Jersey, where he was a supply sergeant. I think it was around World War I. Dad used to say that if one little match was lit, the whole place would blow up," Paul says about the facility, which did blow up in 1926.

"After my father got out of the Army, he worked at New York Telephone and was a baker in Hampstead, New York, at night. He worked two jobs to support us. We had a big family—I had 2 brothers and 3 sisters—and times were hard."

During WW II, Dorothy went to work at Grumman Aircraft in Farmingdale, Long Island. She worked on U. S. Navy Hellcat fighter planes, used in 1942 during the Battle of Midway in the Pacific. "Mom riveted the planes, and my sister, Dorothy (known as "Dottie") worked on the punch press because she lost her wedding finger in a work accident. My sister used to work on the tail end of the plane, and my mother worked on the wing assembly.

"They both had their own tool boxes, and Mom's weighed over 50 pounds," says Paul. "They worked anywhere from 8 to 10 hours a day. They both worked the night shift so they could ride in the same car. I remember her telling me that midgets worked inside the plane's wings doing the riveting because a normal sized person couldn't fit there."

Dottie quit working at Grumman's after the war. Her husband, Al Smith, began working there during the Korean war. "My Mom worked there until she was laid off, then bought the Lucky Star Restaurant at Oyster Bay, near the shipyards. We used to feed the guys who worked in the shipyards during the second war. I remember standing on a 50-pound sack of potatoes, washing pots. I did that five days a week."

Both of the family's Rosie the Riveters are now deceased. Dorothy died in 1980, and Dottie died several years ago. The family cooking skills rubbed off on Paul, who has won numerous culinary awards. Paul joined the Army in 1953, went to school, and cooked for West Point cadets at Washington Hall. He worked as a civilian chef at several facilities, then went to work as a civil service cook at Fort Benning, Georgia, until he retired after 20 years.

Together We Persevere and Conquer

by Viola Gertrude Rector Edwards
Bolivar, Missouri

Viola in 1945 (left) and in 2002 with her brother, Charles Ray Rector, a 30-year Navy veteran

    I was working at Pratt-Whitney defense plant in Kansas City, Missouri when the war ended in August 1945. We made B-25 bomber engines. I was an inspector on cadmium-plated engine parts. At that time there were several defense plants near the Kansas City area, including North American Aircraft, Lake City Ammunition, Sunflower Powder at De-Soto, Kansas and other plants in Wichita.

    I worked the evening shift, 3:00 p.m. to 11:00 p.m. I rode the city bus and street car to and from work. The buses did not run after 11:00 p.m. so when I got off the street car, I had to walk several blocks (approximately ½ mile) to my apartment, which would be unsafe now.

    I had a small second-story apartment consisting of a living room with small couch and chair, a fold-up bed in the wall, a tiny kitchen with an apartment-sized range and table for two, and a half-bath. I shared a refrigerator with girls in the adjoining apartment, two sisters who also worked at the same plant with me. Several girls in my department had husbands in military service.

Before being employed by Pratt-Whitney, I worked for a company that made Army tents in Kansas City, Missouri (Karney-Goudy Manufacturing Co.). My department sewed metal rings onto the finished tents for ropes to go through for tie-down. We used large heavy needles with waxed heavy twine to sew the rings in. We wore a thick leather pad on the palm of our hand and pushed the needle through the heavy canvas with the heel of our hand.

I also worked for a professional garment company that sewed custom-made uniforms. One of our ladies would go to the establishment to take measurements of the recipients so we could make perfectly fitted garments. We made Red Cross, Grey Lady, and student nurse uniforms, dental gowns for students at dental college, and uniforms for Fred Harvey waitresses at Union Railway Station. Our building was beside a hotel where service men were temporarily stationed.

I met and dated a serviceman named Carl, who was from Alabama and stationed at Headquarters next to my work place. We attended theaters and saw *Gone With the Wind* when it first came out. We enjoyed fun times riding the street car across town to Swope Park, a large, beautiful, natural city park of Kansas City, and hiking over the trails. I lost contact with Carl when he was sent overseas.

The day the war ended, there were big celebrations all over the streets of Kansas City with shouting, dancing, and the deafening noise of cars honking. We all thought that now there would be peace and there would be no more wars – sadly, we were wrong.

After the war ended, I immediately enrolled at cosmetology school in Kansas City and received my Missouri license. I married and had two sons. I later attended Kansas University Medical Center and received my nursing license for both Kansas and Missouri. After a lifetime in the health care profession, I am now retired.

Josey the Riveter

by Josephine C. Farruggio Feige
New Holland, Pennsylvania
as told to her daughter, Dolores Gareis

Josephine at work in the 1940's

I was born in Baltimore, Maryland on October 31, 1918. Both my mother and father were immigrants from Sicily. I was the firstborn and spoke only Sicilian until I went to school. By the time I was 14, I had three younger sisters. At this time, tragedy struck. My mother delivered twin girls and died in the process. I had to leave school to take care of the family. I kept house and cooked for everyone. I married Ed, the boy next door, when I was 18 years old. My new husband did not want me to work, but this all changed with the onset of WW II.

When Pearl Harbor was bombed, I was shocked. Many young people that I knew joined up because we were attacked. I got a job in a sewing factory making men's suits. I heard about a job at the Glenn L. Martin factory outside of Baltimore. My husband did not want me to work there because he thought it was not woman's work. I went to interview for the job. There was a man there who knew my husband. I told him not to tell my husband that I was applying for a job, but he did anyway. That night I had a long discussion with my husband, and we both agreed that we must do everything we could to win the war. I became a machinist.

I was given a training course in a vocational school. I worked on tank tops. One person shot the gun for the rivet while the other person "bucked" the rivet (flattened it out). I also drilled holes in metal. I really liked this work because I loved working with my hands. I had to wear special shoes with hard toes. I also had to tie my hair up to keep it away from the machinery. It was required that we should wear slacks. These were the first slacks I ever had. I developed lots of friendships in the factory. My husband was an electrical engineer working in a different building at the same plant.

I drove a car pool with three men and two women. All of us were young and under 20 years old. I had to wake at 4:00 a.m. when I drove car pools. We got to work at 6:00 a.m. Gas was easy to get because I had some friends with extra ration cards. There were some shortages of clothing, so I made clothes for myself. We tried to grow our own food. I planted tomatoes but the rabbits ate them.

After working for some time at the plant, I became pregnant with my first child. I did not let anyone know for a long time, but eventually I had to quit the job. I was very sorry to leave, and the supervisor said I was the best worker there.

Many of my friends who joined the service were killed in battle. It was a sad time for many. Hitler was terrible. Before the war, some of our German-speaking friends thought he was okay and they often talked about him. After the war started, they kept quiet. When the atom bomb was dropped, I was afraid of it and I didn't like to see that happen, but I was glad that no more of our boys had to die. We were all glad the war was over.

After the war, my husband realized that there would be a slowdown at Glenn L. Martin. He took a job with General Electric and stayed there the rest of his career.

A World War 2 Romance

by Margaret Such Fiala
Henderson, Nevada

"Where two services meet"
Camp Shelby, Mississippi, June 1942

The pre-war and the post-war years, I think, are the most vivid and memorable in most Americans' minds. Pre-war, my soldier and I met at a church Christmas dance and dated until he was called to serve his country in 1940.

He came home on furlough as allotted by the service, and in 1942, on my birthday, we became engaged. We decided to wait until the war was over to marry, but, of course, that was a short-lived theory.

The war all over the world was very heavy by this time, so when my fiancé was home on furlough, we decided to get married. Of course, every arrangement was hectic, but we finally got married on Tuesday, November 8, 1943. We had plans to go to a beautiful resort in Wisconsin on our honeymoon, but bam! my now husband was called back to camp on Wednesday, the day after our wedding. We said "goodbye" until November of 1945, when he was discharged from the service with honor.

During the war years, when we were separated, I worked in the steel mill under military contract (Navy) as so many of us "Rosie the Riveters" did. I was so conscientious about my work that even though my hands were "cooked" from the hot steel, steam, and grease, I operated my machine (tube reducer) with my hands bandaged, and worked hard so that my military men would get their ammo (ammunition) for the "ack-ack" guns on the aircraft carriers. It was the most uncanny coincidence that one of my four brothers was on the aircraft carrier, the USS *Intrepid*. Three of my brothers were in the Navy. The fourth, when he reached 18, enlisted in the Army to follow in the footsteps of his brother-in-law, my husband, who was working with the "Wind Talkers" of WW II, and was with them until the end of the war.

I'm very proud to be a "Rosie the Riveter." We did it!

Oklahoma Sisters to Shipway 7

by Thoral Juanita "Neta" Cargill Fields
Bethany, Oklahoma

Left: Neta with her sister Thorval (Neta is on the right) in the 1940's. Right: Neta in more recent years.

I graduated from high school in May 1943. Two weeks later, I'm working at the Kaiser shipyards in Richmond, California. My father was Pastor of the Church of the Nazarene in Poteau, Oklahoma. My aunt and uncle, who worked in the shipyards in Richmond, had come to Oklahoma on vacation. My father and uncle decided that my older sister Thorval and I would go to California to work in the shipyards and to be near our older brother, "George O." He was a sailor stationed at the Navy base in Alameda, just across the bay from Richmond. This left only our 10-year-old brother Gene at home. We rode to California in the back of a pick-up truck that had been fashioned with a tarp over the bed. Three adults rode in the front and six or seven of us rode in the back. I remember how cold it was at night going through the desert in the back of that truck – even in summer!

We drove straight through and arrived in Richmond about 8:00 on a Sunday night. The next morning, Uncle Erve took my sister and me to the shipyards. We were hired as apprentice burners and started to school that day! We joined the union and were issued hard hats and goggles. We bought metal toe boots and long leather gloves. We already knew to put our hair up under bandanas. They taught us how to mix the acetylene and oxygen and to use the proper amount of pressure to cut the metal. Then we practiced cutting metal all day long. We cleaned our tips with tiny drills in order to make a nice clean cut.

The second day we were in school again for more training. By day three, we were journeyman burners and were assigned to Shipway 7 to build Victory and Liberty ships. I earned $1.20 per hour. The first week, I worked 52 hours in 6 days. After everything was deducted (union dues, war chest, hospital, state taxes and Series E war bonds), my take home pay was $40.65. Of this, I paid $12.50 to my uncle for room and board.

We lived 10 blocks from the shipyard. By the time the buses got to us they were always full, so we walked. I worked everywhere on the ship from fore to aft, the smoke stack to the double bottom. I learned to burn tiny galvanized pipes, to 4-inch thick metal where the shaft was attached to the propeller. It was a thrill to see a ship I helped build slide down the skids into the Bay. I loved every minute. We lived in government housing with 2 bedrooms, a large front room, a walk-through kitchen, and a bath. Our household consisted of 11 people: Uncle Erve, my aunt (Mama Pete) and their 5 children, 2 grandbabies, plus my sister and me. However, it did not seem crowded (only the closets were crowded) because 2 or 3 people at any given time were always working. Mama Pete quit working to keep house and care for the babies while their mothers worked. There was always food on the stove at all hours. These were fun, fun days.

By late 1944, the war seemed to be getting better. The husbands of my two cousins returned and the girls left. Uncle Erve returned to Oklahoma. My sister and I lived with another uncle and his wife in Oakland for a few months, then we returned to Oklahoma by train. I went to college in Bethany, Oklahoma.

I was still living in Bethany when I met my husband of 48½ years, J. Frank Fields, Jr. He passed away in November 1999. He was a Marine during the Korean war. We have identical twin sons, Tim and Tom, and a daughter, Tamra. We have five grandchildren, Danny, Denell, Jason, MacKenzie and Joshua. My sister Thorval passed on September 9, 2005.

How I Met My Husband

by Thoral Juanita "Neta" Cargill Fields
Bethany, Oklahoma

Neta and J in the 1950's (left) and in 1998

I met my husband, J. Frank Fields, Jr., on a blind date on Saturday, April 25, 1951. "J" was stationed at Barstow, California. He had come home to Dallas, Texas on leave. J had a sister, a cousin, and a childhood friend, George McFerron, in school at Bethany Peniel College (now Southern Nazarene University) in Bethany, Oklahoma.

I had been working in the shipyards during WW II, but had returned home to Bethany. I was working at the First National Bank. I had already planned to make a job change, and April 25 was my last day at work. I was planning to move to Kansas City, Missouri and stay with my brother and his wife while I looked for work. Shortly after the bank opened that day, George McFerron came in and asked if I would go on a double date with him and his girlfriend. He said his friend J was home on leave from the Marines. I agreed, and that night we went to what was then Fair Park in Oklahoma City. In 1951, girls dressed up for a date. I was wearing high-heeled white pumps and managed to break the heel off. I figured that would be the end of our date, but we came back to my house and I changed shoes and then we went out again. J returned to Dallas on Sunday. I received a post card from J on

Wednesday, April 30, saying he wanted to see me again and was coming back to Bethany. That night I went to church and about halfway through the service, J slipped in and sat down beside me. Since I had already quit my job, we were together all day Thursday. That evening, May 1, J proposed – but I didn't answer. We were together all day Friday, and then Friday evening, May 2, J proposed again – this time I said YES.

On May 2, J's family came to BPC for his sister Rowena's voice recital. J left on May 3 by bus for California. We had agreed to be married in Bethany in about 3 months when he could get another leave. However, when J got back to base, his orders had been changed and he was to leave for Korea very soon. He called and asked me to come out right then so we could be married. I left Oklahoma by bus on May 24 and arrived in Barstow on May 27. We were married June 6, 1951 at the Marine Corps Post Chapel by Chaplain Warren L. Bost. J asked his friend, Bill Friend, and his wife Mary Ellen to stand up with us. We are still friends and keep in touch. We had a very large crowd at our wedding because there were many Marines who couldn't leave base, and they came just to have something to do. J's friends, Ace and Queenie, gave us a small reception.

By this time, J's orders had once again been changed. We stayed in Barstow until November 1951, when J was transferred to the San Diego Marine base as a drill instructor. J did have to finally leave for Korea in March 1953. I stayed in San Diego and worked. J returned from Korea in June 1954 and was Honorably Discharged. We decided to return to Dallas. I became pregnant soon after his return and gave birth to identical twin boys (Timothy Franklin and Thomas Franklin) on May 27, 1955. J was working as a bricklayer, but decided he needed to get an education so that he could get a better job. He had dropped out of school in the 9th grade. So with 4-year-old sons, we moved to Austin where he entered the University of Texas and graduated with a Bachelor of Science degree in Physics. J entered Civil Service and that took us all over the country. Our daughter, Tamra Jill, was born on November 27, 1963 while we lived in Corona, California. On November 22, 1999, two days before Thanksgiving, J passed away instantly of a heart attack. We were married 48½ years.

From School Teacher to Rosie the Riveter

by
Elizabeth "Betty" Fisher

Cottage Grove, Oregon

Betty at age 19

May 1943: I had just finished my first year as a teacher in a one-room school in rural northern Wisconsin. I was 19 years old. I resided with a farm family and walked one and a half miles to the school, where I also did my own janitor work. I was paid $90 a month for teaching, and $5 for doing the other job, which consisted of building the fire in the furnace, filling the water fountain, and of course, cleaning the building.

A friend (also a teacher) and I decided to join the war effort that summer, traveling by train to Cheyenne, Wyoming, where her sister and brother-in-law had assured us of the need for workers there. We got jobs right away working for United Air Lines, modifying B-17 bombers. After several weeks of training, we were put to work installing ball turrets, oxygen lines, etc.

At the time, my boyfriend was stationed at Flagstaff,

Arizona. After numerous calls, he convinced me to take the bus to Tucson where we were married on September 2. Robert was 21 on August 12, and I turned 20 on July 4th.

He did not want me to go back to Cheyenne, so we flipped a coin and I lost. Back to Wisconsin I went, but not for long. As the old World War I song said, "How ya gonna keep them down on the farm, after they've seen Paree?" That goes for girls, too.

A girl from my high school days suggested Chicago, so once again a train took me to that destination. I stayed with this friend and her sister until I got a job for Pullman Aircraft on the south side of Chicago. This is where C-47 wings were made. Once again we went through a training program where we learned how to drill, rivet, and buck rivets. I was put on an assembly line bucking rivets inside the wing. We were paid by the amount we produced, so we were "gung ho" to go. Going from $95 a month to as much as $100 a week was pretty exciting and a lot of money in those days. We were encouraged to buy war bonds on a regular basis, so I had quite a bit saved by the time Robert came back from overseas.

National Archives, Color poster, 1942. 44-PA-531

I worked there until Robert came home after finishing his 50 missions over Europe as a tail gunner on a B-24 bomber. We celebrated our first wedding anniversary in Miami Beach, Florida (his rest and recreation) before being reassigned to Gowan Field, Idaho. I quit my job and joined him there. That was the end of my wartime career.

Those were exciting times and they changed many of our lives forever.

The War Years

by Wanda Duffy Flowers
Norman, Oklahoma

Left: Wanda Duffy, war time years.
Right: Wanda Duffy Flowers, retirement years.

Looking back, I remember that my graduation from high school came after the war had been going on for two years. The boys in the P. E. class were learning to march and do push-ups and other exercises. The girls were included in school drives for aluminum and scrap iron for the war effort. Upon graduation from Eureka (Kansas) High School, two girlfriends and I went to Wichita, Kansas to work in the Defense Plants. Lucy Mae Martin got on the second shift at Boeing and Normalie Brown became a secretary at Boeing (first shift) and I, Wanda Duffy (only 17 years of age), got on the first shift. State law said that all who were 18 years old and under had to be on first shift. I became a riveter at Aero Parts, a subdivision of Boeing. I riveted wings. Aero Parts made Trainer Planes for beginning pilots to learn on.

For a year I riveted, and then four of us were placed in a specialized area. We put flaps on casings that covered the motors. Alma Thiessen was my partner. Her sister, Dorothy Thiessen, worked on the next unit.

I rode to work at Aero Parts in a car pool. I took a bus to a certain corner and was picked up and taken to work. Later I would be returned to the same corner, take the bus and home. Home was a garage apartment. Lucy Mae eventually went back home, and Normalie and I moved to town. I now had a new ride to work – a husband and wife, in their car. They picked me up on the front porch of the new place. I ate at the plant cafeteria.

My total plan was to earn enough money to pay for college. The year of my graduation, my family moved to Ada, Oklahoma. My dad was a gauger for the Sinclair Oil Company and they needed him there. Ada also had a Teacher College.

I did not work until the end of the war, but I did move to Ada and began college. I received a Bachelor of Science degree in Education and married Solomon Flowers, a war veteran. We raised five children. He was a movie projectionist, and I taught school

After 48 years of marriage, I became a widow. After retiring, I've traveled to Europe three times, the Caribbean Islands twice, Mexico, Honduras, Alaska Inside Passage, both coasts of Canada, Hawaii twice, the Holy Land, and Egypt. In 2008, I toured Russia. I have a son who served two tours of duty in Vietnam, and a son that served in Desert Storm in Saudi Arabia. At this date, our country is still at war.

Steel-toed Rosie

by Ava Walton Forrester
Oklahoma City, Oklahoma

Ava Walton Forrester

My husband and I had just bought a house full of new furniture a month before Pearl Harbor was attacked. Sure enough, he was called up, so I had to go to work to pay for that new furniture. My mother took care of Jody, my four-year-old daughter, and I went to work for Douglas Aircraft Company at Tinker Field in Midwest City.

Going to work for Douglas Aircraft was a big job for me. I got through the training process in about three weeks, and was put on the assembly line making the left wing for the C-47 airplane.

After I was there for a while, my lead man put me in charge of "riveting" the skin on the left wing. I got pretty good with that rivet gun. The wing was made on this big "jig" or frame that rolled along a track. I had to wear steel-toed shoes in case my shoe got in the track. Without the steel toe in the shoe, that frame would take your toes right off. I got so good with the rivet gun that when someone got a rivet in wrong or it cracked, I would drill it, remove it, and put in a good one.

Working on that assembly line was hard work but I enjoyed it. It was so loud in there you couldn't hear yourself think. One day, my lead man came by with my check, and he sorta hugged me and said, "Where we going tonight, babe?" I said, "We're not going anywhere anytime." But right as I said that, the noise was shut off, and all the other girls heard what I said and everyone started laughing. Boy, did he turn red. I had been on the morning shift and finally got on the "swing shift," which I liked a lot better.

I am very proud to have been able to help the war effort and proud to be a "Rosie the Riveter."

Douglas C-47 "Skytrains", 12th Air Force Troop Carrier Wing, loaded with paratroopers for the invasion of southern France, August 15, 1944.

My Rosie Experiences

by
Harriet R. Frankel

Atlanta, Georgia

Harriet at her 90th birthday party

Rosie the Riveter is having a convention in Atlanta? Why don't I go? I might see someone I know from so long ago. I won't be able to hear the speakers... hum, hum . . . I'll go anyway. Just the thought stirred up memories.

I started probing my memories of the days and weeks and months I spent as a production illustrator at Bell Bomber plant in Marietta, Georgia. How did it all start? America was in the midst of World War II and the draft was in effect. I had just learned that my husband Norman was 4F because of a heart murmur, so it would be up to me to represent our family. The government was offering women scholarships for college if you joined the WAVES, and I had always wanted to go to college.

I registered to qualify for the WAVES. They wanted me because I was an artist, but when tested for hearing I was rejected. Then I took a test for being a meteorologist, and while waiting for the test results I saw an offer at Georgia Tech for free drafting lessons if you would take a war job. That's for me! I can already draw and I'll be halfway there.

At that time, Georgia Tech didn't take women students. I had always had a hankering to be an architect but didn't qualify due to lack of college and math. This might be my chance.

I was accepted and started an intense course in sheet metal drafting. The class had mostly men who were artists. For them, this was better than being a Private in the draft. I completed the course, passed it, and applied for a job as a draftsman at the bomber plant. For a test, they asked me to do a perspective drawing of a hand meat grinder. They also asked me if I could sew and follow a dressmaking pattern, which I could.

I got the job and joined a car pool to drive to Marietta, Georgia. When we got there, we were sent to the basement of the assembly plant because it wasn't ready yet, but they were hoarding qualified workers for the bomber plant to keep them from taking other offers. When the plant was complete, I started my job. I was not a riveter but was in the engineering department. Our job was to make a drawing that showed what the part would look like when completed, before it was actually made. We made exploded drawings to show the workers how to assemble the parts. The engineers could make isometric drawings, but it took artists to draw the parts in perspective to show what they would look like. Today, if you buy unassembled furniture, there are similar drawings to show you how to put it together. . . where the screws, nuts and bolts go. It was an essential job, since most Georgia workers were farmers and not experienced in reading blueprints.

I was the second woman in that department. The other woman was an architect. I worked on plans for putting extra gasoline in the wings of the B-29 Bomber until I was pregnant with my first child and couldn't get through the turnstiles.

Epilogue: After the war was over and Bell Bomber became the site of Lockheed Aircraft, I applied for a job there as a production illustrator. The response was, "The war is over and we're not hiring women." I got a job as a furniture illustrator, but shortly after, Lockheed called and offered me a job because production illustrators were very scarce. Of course, I turned them down in a very impolite way.

The Post

by
Rochelle Coulombe
Warrenton, Oregon

as told to her
by her mother,
Ruby Gano

Ruby at age 87

After the Japanese attack on Pearl Harbor on December 7, 1941, the defense of the west coast of the United States became paramount. A friend of ours coordinated Civil Defense activities in our county, and he began recruiting volunteers to man observation posts along the coast of Washington. Sites were located in the foothills of the Olympic Mountains and equipped with shortwave radios to report planes or enemy ship sightings. Because of a physical disability, my husband was listed as "4F" and not eligible for military service. Our brothers, nephews, and cousins were enlisted and we wanted to do our part for the war effort, so Dick and I volunteered to accept a post.

On a hot September afternoon in 1942, my parents drove us the 90 miles north of Aberdeen and delivered us to the trail head leading to our new home. We carried our belongings about a half mile up the hill to the location where we would pitch our tent and set up housekeeping for the next several months. Our job, 24 hours a day, was to spot enemy aircraft, and to monitor the air waves for enemy transmissions.

It took us a few days to get our camp site set up. We dug a pit and lined it with canvas to use as a cooler. We cut wood and learned the whims of the small cookstove we installed in the tent. By the time the fall rains arrived, we were settled in to a routine, always remembering that one of us needed to be awake at all times. Our mail was delivered to the trail head, and the mailman would honk to let us know the delivery had been made. Once a week we would put a grocery list in the mailbox, and our nearest neighbor would drive into town and pick up groceries for us.

The days passed without much excitement, other than the occasional bear or elk wandering through camp, but one evening the radio burst into static and we heard Japanese men talking. We were frightened! All kinds of things rushed through our minds. Was this a genuine submarine attack? Remember that this was war time, and there was real fear the Japanese would launch a major attack against our west coast. We radioed headquarters and waited and waited. We never heard any transmissions again, and the conclusion was that enemy submarines were off the coast of Washington, but for whatever reason they never attacked.

There were many civil defense sites along the west coast, managed by citizen volunteers wanting to make a small contribution to the safety of our country. Serving as plane spotters helped us feel included in the war effort.

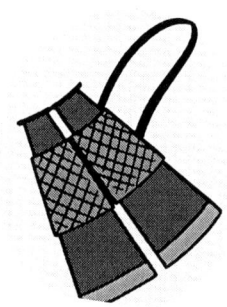

How I Remember It

by Lois Reynolds Gedney
Salem, Oregon

Lois and her husband, Herb, on April 12, 1944

I grew up during the Great Depression in a small town on the Columbia River (The Dalles, Oregon), where I graduated from The Dalles High School in 1942. As in other small towns across the country during this time, jobs were scarce. My girlfriend, Frances Tibbitts, and I had saved some money and were going to Portland, Oregon to see if we could find jobs. It was an exciting time for us and we thought it would be a piece of cake.

We looked and applied at all the stores downtown and other places. The bus driver got to know us pretty well from our daily travels looking for jobs, and one day he told us we should go over to Vancouver, Washington and apply at the Kaiser shipyard.

We were running out of money, so we were hoping to have some luck at the shipyard. The manager (Woody Woodworth) asked if we were 18 years old. We both said yes, though I was still 17. He said he could use two girls to help sign in the bus loads of people that were recruited from all over the country.

We signed them in, took their applications, directed them to different departments, and saw to it that they were fingerprinted. It was a great job and we were so proud to be helping with the war effort. When I did turn 18, the next morning I went straight to Woody's office and told him. He got the biggest laugh out of it. A year later, Woody was best man at my wedding.

Now that Frances and I were working full time and had a

little extra money to spend on entertainment, we would go to downtown Portland to a place called The Music Hall, where a lot of service men would go for some R & R. One Saturday night, I met a good-looking airman from the Portland Air Base who had just returned from the Aleutian Islands. He came over to the table where a bunch of us shipyard girls were sitting, and in the middle of a song he asked me for a dance. When the music stopped, he asked for the next dance and the next and the next. I got a call at work, asking if I would be at the dance the next Saturday, that he would like to dance with me some more. From then on, we only dated each other, and about a year later we were married.

My husband was an aircraft armor and turret specialist on B-17 and B-24 bombers, which they did not have at the Portland Air Base, so we were moved around quite a bit. When my husband's crew was assigned overseas flight duty with the 8th Air Force in Europe, I was pregnant with our first child. I went home to The Dalles and lived with my folks and little sister in a small two-bedroom house, waiting for a letter from my husband with news that he was still alive. He wrote that he had some close calls, but because of the censorship there was very little he could tell me. Our first child was born May 5, 1945. Later I found out that he was on a mission that day dropping surrender leaflets telling people that the Germans had surrendered and what they were to do.

Then my husband was assigned to the 9th Air Force for E-vac and Occupation duty until the Japanese surrendered and he was discharged at Ft. Lewis Army Base in Tacoma, Washington. We met in Portland and spent a week at the old Portland Hotel, where we used a drawer in the dresser for a bed for our baby girl. Then we went on to The Dalles for a big Thanksgiving dinner.

My father-in-law lined up a job for my husband in Boston, Massachusetts, which he hated, and we lived with his folks and his brother. Later, my mother sent word that there was going to be an opening at the Mayflower Dairy Plant in The Dalles for a salesman, and they would hold it open until we could get there.

The housing in The Dalles was very limited. We found a studio apartment, then our name came up for a one-bedroom apartment in a government housing complex. We purchased an old "A" Model Ford until our name came up at one of the car dealers for a newer model car. This is how I remember it after 60 years.

My Life Began a Big Change
by Kate Weeks Grant
Moore, Oklahoma

Below: The Grant family in the 1960's

Above: Kate and Melvin during their dating days, 1942

I told my principal at school and my teacher that I was quitting school. They said that if I would stay and play ball, they would see that I graduated from high school. I said, "No, I won't be back next week." That was kind of them, and I loved school. I was ready to quit farming and working in the hot sun. Friday, March 27, 1942 was the last day.

Early on Saturday morning, March 28, my friend Gereldine and her fiancé Ulas got married. We drove all the rest of the day and night, and went to Belle Vista, California, where Ulas and his brother Melvin had been boarding. Melvin came out to the pick-up. Ulas said, "Melvin, meet my wife Gereldine and her girlfriend, Maggie Weeks."

Melvin reached his hand through the window and shook my hand. I thought, He can't be a farmer, his hands are too soft. And he didn't smell like cow manure. He had on dress pants and a green silk shirt and shined slippers, and

I thought, That's different from the Oklahoma farmer boys. He said it was his 19th birthday, and what a good present it was to meet me! He was a handsome young man.

    We started going places together some. I guess I was so young, 17 and a half years old when we first met, that I was still thinking of playing ball and sports. He would come to see his brother Ulas, as they were still working together and owned the pick-up together. We would go to a show or ride around on rainy days when they couldn't work, as they worked outside. The flowers were so pretty along the highway, and the fruit trees and orange blossoms smelled so good. There was an English walnut orchard behind Jellie and Ulas' cabin at Oakley. We would walk through it and eat walnuts. So this kind of became our walk every time he came over, and he got to where he came more often. We became fond of each other and did not want to be away from each other. We would plan places to go and things to see. Soon we became engaged to be married.

    Melvin and I went to Oklahoma. We went to McAlester and got our marriage license on Monday, November 23, 1942. I bought a pretty blue princess dress with a big pink rose on it from the shoulder down to the waist, and pleats at the bottom. It cost $11.00. I probably got patten slippers and bobbie socks.

    On Wednesday he said that he would be over Thursday night when he got through working in the peanut field. We would be married on Thanksgiving Day, November 26, 1942. We were married in Crowder, Oklahoma at the home of my sister and her husband, Idell and Potter Kirby. Our first apartment was in Crowder and the rent was $2.00 a week. During the war, I worked as a welder at the Richmond shipyard in California.

    We were married for more than 65 great years when Melvin passed away on March 18, 2008. He still had soft hands and was handsome. We still loved each other very much.

The Ones He Left Behind

by Laquetta Grant Brummett
about her mother, Kate Weeks Grant
Moore, Oklahoma

Cousins Leon, Ulas, Eddie, and Laquetta lived together while their mothers worked during World War II.

My Dad served as a U. S. Marine in one of our country's worst battles of World War II, Okinawa, as a special weapons flame-thrower operator. My mother Kate was one of millions of women to enter the American work force in 1943. She became a welder in the Richmond Shipyards #2 in Richmond, California. Mom was one of thousands of women who worked in the Richmond yard.

My Dad shipped out on September 11, 1944. I was 16 months old. Mom and my Aunt Idell rented a 3-bedroom shotgun house in Pittsburg, California. Aunt Idell and her three sons moved in with us when Uncle Potter, serving in the Army, shipped out in October 1944. They split the duties of child rearing while working separate shifts.

Mom worked at the John Mansville Roofing Company

from 8:00 a.m. until 4:00 p.m., and Aunt Idell worked at a fountain serving sandwiches and sodas from 5:00 p.m. until 11:00 p.m. They would pass each other at the gate of the little picket fence that surrounded our house. Aunt Idell took care of us kids—Leon, Ulas, Eddie, and me—during the day, and she would have the washing done, house cleaned, us four kids fed, and dinner ready for Mom. Then Mom would bathe us and put us to bed after lots of stories, and tell us about our Dads and what they were doing for our country. She would do all the ironing, then she tells me that she would write my Dad letters and cry and cry.

One day, Mom returned home from donating blood and found Aunt Idell screaming and crying in grief. Aunt Idell had received a telegram stating that Uncle Potter had been killed in action May 13, 1945 on Okinawa, Japan. Mom said Aunt Idell moved home with Granny and lost touch with the world for about a month. She wouldn't get out of bed and hardly ate. One day she got up and told my Granny that Uncle Potter had come to her in a dream and told her to get up and raise their boys. After that, Aunt Idell returned, and she and my Mom continued working and living in Pittsburg, California.

Pfc. William Kirby

Pfc. William Kirby Killed on Okinawa

Pfc. William P. Kirby, formerly of Crowder was killed in action on Okinawa on May 13. He was the son of Mr. and Mrs. John Kirby, Checotah, and his wife, Mrs. Idell Kirby, and three sons reside at Pittsburg, Calif.

My Dad did come home as a hero to me, and later, my four brothers were born. My Aunt Idell later married a wonderful man, my Uncle Dick. Together they reared three wonderful, high-achieving sons. The four of us were so lucky to have two wonderful hard-working mothers during the war, and we have always been very close.

Hand In Hand

by
Ginevra Boyes

*about her
grandmother,
Kate Weeks Grant*

Moore, Oklahoma

Kate and Melvin on April 9, 1946. Kate's notation reads, "Second day home after the war. A wonderful day for sure."

 One thing I remember vividly, from my earliest memories to now, is my grandparents holding hands. Not in the corny way of young love, or in the particularly romantic way of newlyweds, but in the way of lifelong partners and best friends. I never really knew why, but it always made me feel safe and secure to see it. The occasional clasping of their two hands, no matter how brief, exchanged a lifetime of shared love and said more in that instant than all the words ever written on the subject.
 They were holding hands the first time they spoke to each other through the window of a 1942 Chevrolet pickup. My Grandpa had just been introduced and he shook my Grandma's hand and said, "Today is my 19th birthday, what a great present it is to meet you." Eight months later they were married, and they held hands for more than 65 years.

His hands had been those of a farmer, a CCC worker, and shortly after they wed, they became those of a Marine, carrying a flame-thrower on Okinawa for 83 days. Her hands had been those of the school's star ball player and a dairy farmer's daughter, and while her new husband was fighting in foreign lands, they learned to weld with hot iron in the shipyards of Richmond, California. During the war, my grandparents held hands long distance through letters, from her hand to his and back again. After the war, their hands built a life together, rearing their children with loving hands that were at times hard with the sternness of discipline, but always balanced with encouragement and guidance. They went into the ministry, and those hands together did God's work, praying, sharing, comforting, lending strength, and showing compassion to others, while still holding fast to each other.

One thing I have noticed about holding hands is that it comes most naturally when positioned side by side. Prolonged hand-holding becomes difficult and uncomfortable when one person is always in front of the other, or if the distance between them grows too great, or if the bond becomes strained by an outside force. At the same time, a hand held too tightly becomes unbearable. Somehow, they always seemed to get it right. That simple act of holding hands has taught me more about love and life and a life equally shared with another, than all the sermons, lectures, and life experiences combined. My grandparents, Melvin and Kate Grant, were still holding hands after 65 years of marriage, when he passed away in March 2008, and yes, it still made me feel safe.

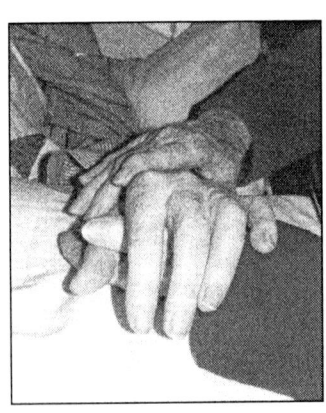

Kate and Melvin were still holding hands when this picture was taken on March 16, 2008, two days before his death.

Dear Diary

by

Dorine Smith Hamilton

Wichita, Kansas

Dorine and Leroy in the 1940's, when she worked at Boeing and he was in the Army

I attended the same high school as my future husband, Leroy. He walked to school in the city, and I rode a school bus from the country. We were married in October 1942. Later that same month, Leroy was called to service in the Army. During the next four years, we would see each other only four times, for a day or two each time.

While Leroy was away, I worked at the Boeing plant in Wichita. I was called a "hand former" because we hand-held blocks to pound out the wrinkles.

Leroy was in the Battle of the Bulge, and he was actually on furlough when the war ended abruptly after the two atomic bomb attacks. I was on leave then, also, to be with him while he was on furlough. After the war, because Leroy had not served long enough, he was transferred to Camp Cook, California, to finish his military requirement.

Leroy was discharged in 1946. We loved to ride motorcycles. People would ask, "Do you have children?" and my reply was, "We have motorcycles." I worked for the Department of Defense and was a member of the National Motor Maid Association. Leroy was killed in an accident in 1964.

In 1960, I entered the Top Ten Popular Rider Contest, determined by club votes. I rode to Daytona Beach. Upon my return home, I wrote about my experiences for *Cycle Magazine*. Following are some short quotes about the trip:

Saturday: Left for Daytona.

Sunday: "D Day": Damp Drizzle, Dangerous Dogs, Delinquent Drivers.

Monday: Drove to the O'Quinns in Jacksonville. My namesake was a buddy rider to Daytona.

Tuesday: Two beauties cut the opening ribbon. Why not a Motor Maid?

Wednesday: Rode to Bellair Plaza to parade, but there was insufficient attendance. I rode the route, and where there were mothers with children, I stopped to talk. I flattered myself that one rider stopping to talk was as good as a group quickly riding by.

Dorine and Leroy getting ready for a motorcycle ride. Dorine's comment today is, "Mercy! You see why I have to go to the dermatologist!"

Thursday: Went to the bandshell on the boardwalk for the trophy presentation. I was 7th. At least I had the opportunity to thank my sponsoring clubs.

Friday: Took our friend Otto out on the town.

Saturday: Took my nieces to Sea Zoo, where they rode in a rowboat pulled by a porpoise.

Sunday: Attended the Motor Maid breakfast. I was awarded the Long Distance Trophy (1,427 miles). Used the Top Ten gift to attend the 200 Miler. Leroy and I started home, and down came liquid sunshine! Makes you think of the old saying, "A poor beginning means a good ending." It really was good to get home!

Rosies Pave the Way for New Careers

by
Gar-Fay Harrison

Corvallis, Oregon

Gar-Fay in 1943

After graduation from high school in May 1943, I went to Portland, Oregon, where the shipyards were. My brother was employed there, and I got a job stenciling ID numbers on steel plates that were used in building the ships. After the ships were completed, all employees gathered to witness the christening with a champagne bottle. That was usually swung by a dignitary from Washington, D. C. I witnessed many launchings during my employment.

After about 15 months, I moved to Boise, Idaho, where I was employed with the IRS. I volunteered with the USO where we sold many savings bonds and stamps, and were called Minute Maids. Through that service we were hostesses at Gowan Field in Boise, and Mountain Home Army Air Field (now Mountain Home Air Force Base) near Boise. We danced with the GI's, accompanied live by great bands of the 40's, including Glenn Miller, Les Brown, and singer Doris Day. It was a wonderful experience for a young girl, and I have many happy memories.

In August 1945, I married Stanley Harrison, a young Air Corps Lieutenant, who served as a Bombardier. He was in Alamogordo, New Mexico, being present for the atomic bomb test known as "Trinity." After his discharge and the end of the war, he went to Utah State University under the GI Bill. Stan was recalled in 1951 due to the Korean War. Although he reported for duty, he was not accepted due to our daughter's polio. We raised five daughters and two sons. We moved to Corvallis, Oregon, after he received his Master's degree. He taught school for many years. Stan died on May 22, 2008.

Just a few days ago, my close friend, Dru Rowe, was telling about how she recently found out that she was a Rosie. I asked what the qualifications were, and we both laughed when I said, "I'm a Rosie, too." Upon recounting our amazingly parallel experiences on opposite coasts, we both agree that ALL Rosies opened up a large number of new employment opportunities. Back in the 1940's, the usual jobs available for women were teacher, housemaid, nurse, or secretary. So we Rosies should all be proud of our contributions – both to our World War II effort, and to a future of diverse careers for women!

Gar-Fay in 2008

Reunited in Yosemite

by Carol Peters
Maxwell, Texas
about her mother, Anniece Aikins Hawkins

Left: The upstairs apartment where Anniece and Leonard started their married life. Center: The Hawkins family in 1960. Right: Anniece and Leonard's last snapshot in 1991.

My parents got married six months before Pearl Harbor Day, and Anniece Aikins became Anniece Hawkins at age 20. Two years before, my dad, Leonard Hawkins, and a friend were out cruising around when Dad decided they should go visit an old girlfriend of his. Marion called her friend Anniece who, after initially declaring that her hair was in curlers, agreed to come along as the blind date of Dad's friend. Later, Dad asked his friend if he'd mind Dad inviting Anniece on a date himself, which resulted in their wedding on June 5, 1941.

After honeymooning on a stern-wheel passenger boat on Lake Erie with an overnight stay at the Book Cadillac Hotel in Detroit, they moved into an upstairs apartment in Ashtabula, Ohio for $17 per month. On June 15, 1942, Dad was drafted, and rather than sleep in a trench, he decided to enlist in the Navy and was shipped out to basic training. Mom told of journeying by train to Florida and then to New York City to visit her husband before he was shipped out to the South Pacific.

Mother moved back home to live with her parents, soon finding a job at the Farmer's Bank, replacing a male who had enlisted in the service. There she was trained as a bank teller and sold war bonds, often accepting coins saved by school children to buy bonds that would help the country supply ships, planes, tanks, and ammunition for the war.

I can only imagine why Mom decided to become a Rosie by going to work at the bank. When her 23-year-old husband of only twelve months left to go to war near Japan, I am sure that she felt lonely, maybe angry and deserted. However, she also probably wanted to help the country fight for their safety. She had some business training and her German/British parents had always preached working hard, saving money, and showing patriotism. So, in 1942, when she heard that they needed help at the bank since so many men were signing up to fight, she probably thought it would be an opportunity to keep busy and keep her mind off the danger her husband was in.

When my father was injured in late 1944, my mother immediately quit her job at the bank and took a train to California to be with him during his recovery. After he was released from the hospital, they lived in a cabin in Yosemite National Park while he continued to recover from the trauma he had experienced since he had drowned and then been resuscitated.

About June 1945, my father was reassigned to a Navy base in Columbus, Ohio. Mom was able to live with him there. I was born in February 1946. After the war, my parents bought a house in Ashtabula with a GI loan, and Dad got a job at the local electric utility plant while earning an associates degree in accounting under the GI Bill. My mother stayed home to care for me and my brother, who came in 1948. She later returned to work at the Farmer's Bank in 1954, retiring in 1977.

They celebrated their 50th anniversary on June 5, 1991. Mom passed in 1992 on the birthday of her firstborn child. I've often wondered since then about that coincidence, and how important that date must have been to her after three years of wondering if Dad would return from war so they could start a family at all.

I Was a Tinker Belle

by Zola Walton Heck
Oklahoma City, Oklahoma

Zola (left) with her twin sister, Zona.

It was a beautiful Sunday afternoon. My friend and I had just come out of seeing a movie, when we heard all the commotion about the bombing of Pearl Harbor. At that time I was working at a clothing store in downtown Oklahoma City. As the months went by, I felt like I was not contributing to the war effort, then I got the opportunity to go to work for Douglas Aircraft Company at Tinker Air Force Base. Thus I became, along with my twin sister Zona and my sisters, Ava and Violet, not only an airplane builder, but a "Tinker Belle." I worked at Tinker from 1942 to 1945.

While my brother Marvin was an officer in the Navy, my sisters and I jumped at the chance to work for Douglas Aircraft Company, but found the work very hard. My job was putting the self-sealing gel into the gasoline wing tanks of the C-47 airplane. My sister Ava built the left wing of the C-47 and my sister Violet got a secretary job. The

Douglas building was a mile long, so once we got to work we never saw each other. I was finally promoted to the blueprint department, a job more to my liking.

Zola Walton Heck

During my employment with Douglas Aircraft, I met my future husband, Max Heck. He was a C-47 check pilot and inspector. We were married in 1944.

It was an exciting time of my life, and even though everyone was working long hours for the war effort, and sealing wing tanks was a messy job, it was very satisfying knowing we "Rosies" were helping to win the war. It was a great feeling to see all those C-47 airplanes roll out the door, and know that I had a part in building them.

The Douglas C-47 Skytrain
was a cargo and troop carrier.

Jean's Story - Badge #247

by Jean M. Holloway
Charlotte, North Carolina

Jean and Ed in June 1944 (left) and more recently

Our romance started in April 1944. I was a senior in high school and Ed had just signed up for service in the U. S. Navy. Ed went to boot camp in Sampson, New York. I graduated high school on June 4, 1944, and applied for a clerk's job in Watson Flagg Machine Company in Paterson, New Jersey, as a Time and Material Clerk. I was hired right away, as I was 18 years old and could work nights. I was hired to work in the same department that Ed had just left, the gear cutting and finishing department. I was a Time and Material Clerk out on the working floor, but I also did office work. They cut gears for PT boats for the Navy, making me a Rosie the Riveter. I earned 80 cents an hour, working 48 hours a week.

I had to take two buses from Little Falls, New Jersey to Paterson. I had a small office, and every hour I had to go around to the machines and record the job pieces cut or scraped, and put a move order on finished pieces. I worked the swing shift every two weeks – 8:00 to 6:00, or 9:00 to 7:00. We had to wear slacks, and that was when women wore dresses more than slacks.

Ed became a sight setter and gunner in the Armed Guard Division of the Navy, making the famous Murmansk (Russia) Run in the North Atlantic. On his first port leave in October 1944, he proposed, and we were married in January 1945. Thirty-six hours after our wedding, his leave was cancelled, and he went to France on *our* honeymoon – I went home.

July 1945 was Victory In Europe. I worked until V-E Day. The plant closed and I went on unemployment - $26 a week for 52 weeks. Ed came back to the States and then was sent to Japan as part of the occupation forces. He had the points to come home. We started our life together. Ed took a job as a big city fireman for 28 years, and then was a volunteer fireman for 12 years – a total of 40 years. From the start of our marriage, I spent many lonely nights worrying if he was coming home or was injured on the job, which did happen several times. I guess being a Navy wife prepared me for being a fireman's wife.

In 1975, we had an auto accident that changed our lives. I spent six weeks in the hospital, and Ed spent five months in a body cast, and a year out of work. Ed could no longer do fire duty, so he retired. We moved to North Carolina and for the last 30 years we have enjoyed life with family, friends, church, and have volunteered together for mission trips and Red Cross disaster teams.

I joined the American Rosie the Riveter Association, and Sharon, Doris, and Amanda are all Rosebuds (female descendants of Rosies). Now at 81 years old, we enjoy each other. Sure we disagree, but that's life. We had three children, six grandchildren, and five great-grands. Through thick and thin and with faith in God and in each other, we stand tall in our love.

Twin Rosies – Double Trouble

by Michael Horton
about his mother, Ruth Hutchens Horton
and his aunt, Ruby Hutchens Taylor
Wagoner, Oklahoma

Twins Ruby Taylor (left) and Ruth Horton were recognized during a half-time ceremony at a University of Oklahoma basketball game in 2007.

Mazie, Oklahoma twins, Ruth Hutchens Horton and Ruby Hutchens Taylor, were double trouble during World War II. From 1942 through 1945 they worked at the munitions powder plant in Chouteau, Oklahoma, Spartan Aeronautics in Tulsa, Oklahoma, and Tinker Air Force Base in Oklahoma City, Oklahoma.

While at Tinker, they worked on B-29 airplanes, rebuilding altimeters and compasses. We often hear of the skill of our pilots as they achieved air superiority during the war. Little is said about the hands and minds of the Rosies who ensured properly working instruments and other equipment, significantly contributing to that superiority. Both twins did their share of riveting. In addition, Ruth did some extra nasty and itchy work, on hands and knees, running electrical wiring through the aircraft's crawl tunnel. Together with all the other Rosies, the twins did the manufacturing work needed to win the war. The German and Japanese leaders obviously thought they could defeat our military (bad mistake), but that is in part because they did not account for the skill and determination of our Rosies.

In addition to being trouble for our enemy, Ruth and Ruby were trouble on the home front as well. Both had  been star basketball players for the Mazie High School Mustangs. Mazie is located about 50 miles east of Tulsa. In the six-player, half-court style of women's basketball at the time, Ruth was a forward and Ruby a guard. During the war, Tinker AFB sponsored a women's basketball team, the Bombers, which competed throughout the state against college teams like Oklahoma Baptist University and Southern Nazarene University. The Bombers coach was Hall of Fame baseball pitcher Allie Reynolds. Legend has it that the Bombers were undefeated.

Prior to working at Tinker, Ruth had married Corporal Frank M. Horton of Celeste, Texas, who went on to be a highly decorated soldier fighting in Europe, surviving the Battle of Hurtgen Forest and the Battle of the Bulge. While at Tinker, Ruby met and married her husband, Air Force Sergeant Jimmy Taylor of Mt. Pleasant, Texas.

Still double trouble, the twins reside in Wagoner, Oklahoma, where they are enthusiastic basketball fans, are active in their churches, are having fun with their families, and are enjoying celebrity status at the local Curves gym.

GI Joe won the battles. Rosie won the war.

High School Sweethearts

by Gladys Marley Eckels Jayme
Banning, California

Gladys and George in 1941

We were high school sweethearts and graduated from Fullerton High in 1940 at Fullerton, California. George went to work in aircraft, and I went to Sacramento to my aunts, to take care of my two nephews. I was paid $15 a month plus room and board. After a couple of months, George drove his Model A Ford to Sacramento and brought me back to Fullerton.

We got married and bought a house near Douglas Aircraft in Long Beach. After Pearl Harbor Day, George enlisted in the Army Air Force and I moved back with my parents. My mother and I both worked at Douglas Aircraft as "Rosie the Riveters" on the B-17 Bombers. We crawled in and out of planes, riveted bulkheads, drilled out imperfect rivets, ate sack lunches, and got paid $33 a week. The fear of enemy attack in California was so great, all defense plants were camouflaged. The whole parking lot at the plant was covered with netting.

I worked for about a year as a "Rosie," then followed my husband and worked at the PX on Army bases in New Mexico and Washington state. When George returned from Okinawa after the war, we raised our two children. He is now deceased.

Our son Rodney, now a Vietnam war veteran, works in construction in Grass Valley, California. Our daughter Diane is co-owner of a construction management company for the California school district in Yucaipa, California. I do volunteer work at the Senior Center for the city of Banning, write books about our family history, and enjoy being with my family whenever I can.

Great Grandma Gladys with Madisen, Christmas 2007

Our Marriage Was Meant To Be

by
Jonnie Melillo Clasen

*about her friend,
Jean Graham Johnson
Columbus, Georgia
and Jean's mother,
Jean Graham*

Jean and Cam
on their wedding day

Jean Graham was waiting for surgery at Warm Springs, Georgia, when she met Campbell "Cam" Jackson Johnson Jr., who had just been discharged from the U. S. Marine Corps and was a survivor of the bitter battle at Iwo Jima.

"My parents had retired here in Columbus (Georgia)," says Jean. "It was 1945, and I was waiting to be called for surgery." Stricken with polio as a young girl, Jean's first surgery was when she was 13 years old.

"I knew Cam's parents long before I knew him," says Jean. "They introduced me. I had been in and out of their house many times before he came back from the service. We all went to the same church.

"Cam was always so kind to his parents, especially his mother, and he was very nice to me. It was just something that was meant to be. We knew each other for three years, and were engaged for two years."

An Army brat and only child, Jean was born in Washington, D. C. She grew up in a family of medical practitioners. Her father, Otis, was an Army doctor in both World War I and World War II. "Mother, who was a registered nurse, was from Canada," says Jean. Her parents, who married in 1915, met in Chicago when her father was attending medical school and her mother was a student at Michael Reese Hospital.

Before returning to Columbus, both Jean and her mother (also named Jean) worked at the Willow Run Bomber Plant, which made B-24 aircraft at its facility about 15 miles from Ypsilanti, Michigan. "I started working there in July 1943, and stayed until February 1944. Mother was a riveter, and then they made her an inspector. Even though she was a nurse, she wanted to do her part for WW II." Jean says that the plant management wanted to use her mother on one of its patriotic promotional posters, but her mother didn't want her face on the poster, so she stood behind what was being riveted.

Jean with her mother. Both of them served as Rosies during the war.

Her father, wanting to retire at Fort Benning, brought the family back to Columbus, where she met Cam in 1945. "Before surgery, I wore long braces when I walked. After the surgery, I had canes. I could barely hobble down the aisle when Cam and I got married. My marriage to Cam and the birth of my son, Campbell Jackson Johnson III, are probably the most significant things that have happened in my life," says Jean, who was also a teacher for 33 years at Winterfield Elementary School before retiring.

Cam, who worked at Shannon Hosiery Mills and in construction, had a great sense of humor and was a people person. "He was a Gideon, one of the people who distribute Bibles," says Jean. "I think he enjoyed being a member of that organization more than his church work. He was just barely 60 when he died."

Jean looks at life as an adventure, from volunteering at the USO in 1943, when she received a 500-hour pin, to riding on the back of her son's motorcycle until she was 85. In 2008, she was at the grand opening of the first USO in Columbus, Georgia since WW II.

Kentucky Lightnin' Strikes Twice

by Willie Lou Moore Mitchell Kidd
Athens, Georgia

Willie Lou in 1946 in
Owensboro, Kentucky

I turned 21 years old in 1942 and left home (Weir, Kentucky), moved to Owensboro, Kentucky, and got a job at the Kenrad Corporation, which made radio filaments for the bombers. I worked there until December 1943. Then I quit and went to work at the Grand Central Hotel as a waitress.

While working at the Grand Central Hotel, I looked up to see a new customer (in an Army Air Corps uniform with beautiful blue eyes) that I had never seen before, and lightnin' struck my heart. He sat at my table and got the best service I could give. He came back when he was home on furlough and finally asked me out after work. I was in heaven!

In May 1944, I received a letter from the Governor of Kentucky saying that my contribution was needed for the war effort, and would I please return to my job at the Kenrad Corporation. I worked there until February 1945, when I quit and went to work at Briggs and Stratton Airplane Company, where I attached landing lights to the wings of bombers.

After the war ended, my "soldier-boy" finally came home, and we got married in February 1947. My husband and I moved to Athens, Georgia in 1959, and he died in 1965.

I remained a widow until 1999, when I was struck by lightnin' again! I married a wonderful gentleman who had been stationed at Camp Breckenridge, Kentucky (not far from Owensboro, Kentucky) before being shipped out to fight in the Battle of the Bulge. He often talks about the tour buses that brought visitors to Camp Breckenridge to say goodbyes to the soldier-boys before they shipped out. Little did he know, but I was on one of those buses and saw this cute, red-headed soldier-boy, and little did I know at the time that we would move to Georgia and he would be the one I would love in my later years.

Who says that lightnin' doesn't strike twice? I am living proof!

Willie Lou with her husband, Fred Kidd, in 2004, Athens, Georgia

It's Been a Long, Long Time

by Lorraine Koop Lazerus
Moorpark, California

Lorraine, as she appeared in a newspaper article in 1945. The caption read, "Former school teacher from South Dakota, pretty Lorraine Koop, 23, measures a shaft which she is grinding at the 12th Avenue vocation school. After three months training—for which she is paid— Miss Koop will take a position as mechanic at the Seattle port of embarkation, which referred her to the school for training."

My role in the war effort began in 1942 in Mitchell, South Dakota, where the local Ford dealer converted his business into a machine shop. We made airplane parts for larger plants. I operated a metal lathe and a precision grinder.

When a friend of mine was going to California to be near her husband who was stationed there, I decided to join her. Douglas Aircraft hired me to work in their precision inspection department. Working there was great except for one incident. When I was assigned a large order of parts to inspect, I found every part had a hole in it that had not been drilled to blueprint specification. I rejected the entire order. A number of workers were quite upset with me. They told me that the parts had been going through that way for a long time and that a bushing was inserted on the assembly line to correct the mistake. That made no sense to me. I stood my ground. Fortunately, my supervisor backed me. The machines were reworked and set to the proper specification. The parts then came through per blueprint. I think we all felt better after that. At least I could, with a clear conscience, face anyone who was serving in the military, including my three brothers in the Army, Navy, and Air Corps.

Meanwhile, my older sister, who was in Seattle, was insisting that I come there. In July of 1945 I arrived and immediately signed up for a machine shop course offered by the Seattle Port of Embarkation. Upon completion, I was assigned to a job at the Port. Before long I heard a lot of girl talk about a certain Lt. Don Lazerus. I told myself, "This Lt. Lazerus must think he's pretty hot stuff." Then on payday, as I was leaving for home, paycheck in hand, someone said, "Now that you got paid, where are you taking me?" I turned and looked into a friendly face with a huge smile. Lt. Lazerus! Since I had just seen my first ice hockey game the previous night, I quipped, "Oh, maybe to an ice hockey game," and I continued out the door.

Lt. Lazerus and I were married less than three months later. "It's Been a Long, Long Time" was our favorite song. Some said it wouldn't last, and sure enough, it ended 55 years, 5 months, and 2 days later, when Don lost his battle to a prolonged illness. We raised three sons and two daughters, who became interesting, caring, accomplished adults. They and their spouses and my grandchildren are my dearest friends.

A World War 2 Love Story

by Dorothy "Lucy" Case Lewis
Birmingham, Alabama

Left: Lucy at age 18 in the 1940's.
Right: A photo of Robert, taken in England in 1944

I was 15 years old and a student at Ensley High School in Birmingham, Alabama in 1941. The State Fair was in town and I had planned to go with several of my friends and my two sisters. One of my friends called and said that Robert Lewis, a boy that I knew, wanted me to go to the Fair with him. I was not too happy about it, but he insisted and we went. I had planned a good time with my friends. They said that he said, "She is the girl that I am going to marry." I hadn't dated many times, and usually it was with my sisters and their friends. I was so young. One of my sisters was four years older than me, and the other was two years older. We were very close and had lots of fun together.

Robert was out of school and working for U. S. Steel, but he did not have a car so we went on a streetcar. We had fun at the Fair, and afterward we went to the end of the streetcar line and back. I still have some things he bought me that night. I think I fell in love with him that night.

The next time he came, he brought me a record player, and we liked to listen to the music together. There was no TV then.

We dated about six months. World War II was in progress and we knew that he would have to go into the service. My sister's boyfriend was already in the Army in Leesville, Louisiana. She planned to be married in February of 1942, and she wanted us to be there. We went, and Robert and I decided to get married at the same time. We had a double wedding.

We knew that he would be drafted and he was, in October of 1942. I really missed him and didn't hear from him often. He never had a leave until he came home three years later.

Robert and Lucy in the 1940's

Robert came home in October of 1945, and we both had grown up, he being in the service and me working, making parachutes, while he was gone. It was so wonderful the day I saw him in Atlanta, Georgia, where he got his discharge. It was like getting married all over again. I was so thankful that he came home safe and we were together again. We came home to Birmingham, Alabama on a train and when we got to Birmingham, we rode the streetcar to our home.

We had 59 wonderful years together and had one son after the war. Robert passed away in June of 2001 of cancer. Our son, who was a medical doctor, died of cancer in 2003.

Being a Rosie helped me through some difficult times after Robert passed away, and I have enjoyed every minute of my work in the organization (American Rosie the Riveter Association).

I am proud to be a Rosie. God Bless America.

James Was a Blessing In My Life

by Jonnie Melillo Clasen
about her mother's cousin, Thelma Aides Fuller Linch
Eatonton, Georgia

Left: Thelma (standing) in the 1940's, with her daughter, Ann, and her cousin, Frankie Melillo, also a Rosie. Right: Thelma and James.

Thelma Aides Fuller Linch, 86, is "thankful for every day" of the 42 years that she worked at Enterprise Aluminum Company in Eatonton, Georgia. It was there that she renewed an acquaintance with a young widower, James Linch, who became her second husband. A fellow employee, James worked briefly in Enterprise Aluminum's garage after returning from WW II with shrapnel in his legs, following his discharge from the U. S. Navy. "He didn't work at the aluminum plant for very long," says Thelma.

Before WW II, Enterprise Aluminum had been making "drip-o-lator" coffee pots, tea kettles, frying pans, saucepans, and other cookware. It converted for the war effort, and began producing canteens, cups, fins for bombs, and other military items. "James said the aluminum company wasn't for him, and he went into business for himself," explains Thelma. However, he worked there long enough for a whirlwind courtship of

Thelma, which resulted in a marriage that lasted "50 years and one day."

"James was a blessing when he came into my life," says Thelma. "I had a blind date with him in February and married him in May. We were married in Eatonton and went to Macon for one night on a honeymoon. I had on a blue dress, and I thought I was something."

But Thelma's life could have taken a different direction. After her first husband, Alvin Fuller, died, leaving her with the responsibility of providing for their young daughter, Ann, some coworkers at Enterprise Aluminum decided to help her out. Unbeknownst to Thelma, some women in the press room wrote her name and address on a piece of paper and stuffed it into a canteen being shipped overseas to the troops. After Thelma and James were married, she received a letter from the young Army soldier who received that canteen. "James told me that I should write to that soldier, which I did, and tell him that I was married now," says Thelma, adding, "To this day, I still don't know which women put my name in that canteen."

Thelma says that James was "the best thing that happened to me and Ann." Thelma and James had a son, Arthur, who today operates the same automotive business his father started many years ago. Thelma believes that she and James were meant to be together. Her first husband and James's first wife died on the same day and are buried in the same cemetery in Eatonton.

It was James's love and that of her young son, Arthur, that helped console her when she lost her daughter, Ann, at age 11 to a battle with acute leukemia. Tragedy wasn't a stranger to Thelma, however. Her mother, Lenore Thompson Aides, was killed in a tragic automobile accident when Thelma was only 5 years old. Thelma was reared by her very resilient and much-loved grandmother, Etta Lou Rhodes Thompson, who had already raised ten children of her own after her husband died, plus seven of her husband's children from his first marriage.

"I had a hard time growing up, and I miss James every day of my life," says Thelma. "He was always trying to help people, and would do anything to help someone. We were very involved with the Veterans of Foreign Wars, and his photo is on the wall of the VFW in Eatonton."

World War 2 Experiences

by Wilma Mathauser Rees
Sun City, Arizona
about her mother, Emma Mathauser

Emma, when she worked at the Cornhusker Defense Plant in Grand Island, Nebraska in the 1940's. This was the first time Emma had ever worn slacks. She wrote on the back of the photo, "Isn't this awful? By our door, last Sat. morning when I came home."

My mother, Emma Mathauser, was 45 years old in 1945. She and my father were living in the small town of Burwell, Nebraska. Their oldest daughter was working in Washington, D. C. for the War Department. Their two younger daughters were both in Seattle and working at Boeing Aircraft, helping to build B-17 airplanes.

Their only son, Elmer, who was in the Army Air Corps, had been reported missing in April of 1942. He was on a special mission flying in a B-17 from Tampa, Florida to Miami. Elmer was a mechanic and not required to fly, but he loved flying and had signed up for this mission. After a few weeks of searching the Everglades and the Gulf of Mexico, the Army accepted the fact that all ten crew members had perished, but my mother never gave up hope of finding her son.

It seemed that a lot of Burwell people were moving to Grand Island and finding jobs to help in the war effort, so my folks decided to try their luck and move to Grand Island, too. They found an apartment in a private home, and Dad found a job in Maintenance at the airport. Mom found a job at the Cornhusker Defense Plant, helping to make bombs! This was certainly something new for her. She had to wear slacks to work. She had never worn slacks before. She had to wear steel-toed shoes. I don't know what her job was, but she was a hard worker and I'm sure she did what was expected of her. However, she was allergic to the powder, and after a short time she had to quit her job. She was a Practical Nurse and got a job in a Grand Island hospital. This was the kind of work she really enjoyed. The folks found a nice apartment within half a block of the hospital. Mom stayed with this job until World War II was over.

The folks moved back to their home in Burwell. Mom kept on being a nurse and was 70 years old before she retired. She lived to be 95 years old.

My Rosie Days
by Helen Mayernick
Dallas, Texas

Helen Mayernick

In 1943, I was just out of high school, and my sister and her husband encouraged me to come to Detroit, where jobs were at a "high" in all the war plants. And so I left West Virginia and became a Major Inspector at Packard Aircraft. The three of us worked the ten-hour night shift and four hours on Saturday.

It was during that time that all parts inspected were stamped to identify the day or night shift work, should any problem arise regarding the parts inspected – and it happened.

Working the night shift meant that our social life was conducted after we left work. Most places of entertainment catered to the night shift workers so we were delighted to attend the "big band" shows, go to movies, or whatever, for our pleasure.

I must add that I enjoyed working with that fine group of people. I worked there until shortly before the war ended. I returned to Weirton, West Virginia to work at the Gas Company, then on to Houston, Texas, Los Angeles, California, and back to Texas. Presently I reside in Dallas, Texas as a retiree from a major oil company after 31 years. Among other interests, I'm a "red hatter."

I'm MOST PROUD to have contributed in a small way to the victory of our grand country!

My only brother, now deceased, served under General Patton, and thank God he returned home safely.

Left: Helen Mayernick, who worked as a Rosie at Packard Aircraft.

Right: Take off from the deck of the USS Hornet *of an Army B-25 on its way to take part in first U.S. air raid on Japan.*

Operating Room Romance

by Elaine G.. Manthey McCray
Pine Mountain Valley, Georgia

*Gene and Elaine on their wedding day,
November 15, 1942*

While standing on a corner in downtown Baltimore, waiting for a streetcar, I heard the newspaper lad shout, "Pearl Harbor bombed by Japanese! President Roosevelt declares war against Japan today, December 7, 1941!"

So far from my Beloit, Wisconsin home, but I had to complete my education at South Baltimore General Hospital School of Nursing. I graduated in April 1942 as a Registered Nurse. Then I and my parents, who had come for graduation, headed home to Beloit.

After settling in, I applied for work at Beloit Municipal Hospital. During the interview I was asked, "What department do you like best?" I quickly replied, "The operating room is my favorite."

"It just happens that we have an opening in that department," answered Miss Johnston, the Hospital Administrator. "Let's go up there now."

While making introductions, Miss Johnston said, "And this is Gene McCray, our Surgical Assistant." Oh! What beautiful blue eyes this dark-haired young man had, and a smile that went straight to my heart! I thought I would be in heaven getting to work with such a handsome man. I learned that when Gene's draft number had come up, Miss Johnston had personally contacted his draft board and pleaded with them not to take him, as she was "trying to run a hospital and could not spare this man." They deferred him.

We worked side by side in the months ahead. He was always kind and polite to everyone, and very patient. He didn't curse, smoke, or drink, was faithful to his church, and had a great sense of humor, all traits I admired.

When we started dating, without a car, courting took place with me sitting on the crossbar of his bicycle. We liked tennis, bowling, swimming, and horseback riding. I enjoyed teaching Home Nursing classes to local homemakers for the Red Cross.

As our relationship grew, we tried to be discreet at work. We would write notes at night, then put them under the operating table pillows in the morning. Then, while passing at work we'd say, "Room A (or B or C)." And no one ever knew.

After five months, he proposed. When he told Miss Johnston he was getting married, and to whom, she was very surprised. Hospital policy stated that husband and wife could not work in the same department, but she said, "If you two have come this far without me hearing about it, I see no reason to separate you two now." We were married November 15.

In December, I transferred to Fairbanks Morse, where, because of the war, they started making diesel engines for submarines instead of manufacturing industrial precision scales.

We were blessed with three children. There is so much more to tell of this World War II romance, but how can you put 55 years of love and life into so few words? Gene died in October 1997, but "Rosie" Elaine, at 85, is still riveting all the beautiful memories together.

Rosie the Riveter

by Kenley Minchew
about her friend, Eloise Snow McMillan
Vinton, Virginia

Left: Eloise in 1943. Right: Eloise (on the right) with her friend, June Pearce, when they worked at Convair Aircraft in San Diego, California, April 1943.

When I met Eloise, she was visiting a long lost friend in Baton Rouge. She stood tall and confident with a strong frame and keen mind. Eloise was born January 23, 1921, on a huge farm in the little town of Waukon, Iowa. Straight out of high school, she began her routine that was going to become her life. She milked cows, cleaned floors, and washed clothes. There were no opportunities awaiting her outside of Waukon, until things suddenly changed due to the war.

Eloise told me how she was sitting in her favorite local café when she overheard that Pearl Harbor had been bombed. "I was devastated!" she said. A week later, she received a letter from her brother Curtis in California, saying jobs were being offered in the Army defense plant. She was not going to pass up the opportunity of a lifetime to get out of Iowa and explore her great nation, which was now entering war. Eloise was only 21 years old when she and her best friend left their hometown for the first time. In 1942, they moved to San Diego to work in an aircraft factory. Scared, yet determined to make it on their own, they traveled by train, which took them five long days and nights. "Weren't we brave? Two small-town girls in a place like that!"

Anxious to begin working, they went directly to the office to fill out an application. After getting their pictures and fingerprints taken, they were told to report the next day, ready to work. With hair tied back, closed toe shoes, and coveralls, they immediately began work. "They made us wear safety glasses. We didn't look too sexy, but we did get a few whistles." The transition was hard but men soon realized that the war would be won at home only with the help of women. "We were really kind of excited about what we were doing," she says. "We knew it was important!" Today, an 8-hour work day from 9 to 5 with a lunch break is considered "hard work." Well, not for these 6 million women. They often worked until 11 at night with no break.

"When I first got there, I did some riveting on panels," says Eloise. "I didn't like the rivet gun too much." Eloise helped assemble bombers. She was reassigned to work on B-17's, the "Flying Fortress," which were the new planes that were going to turn the war around. Her job progressed to an electrician who strung wires from the tail of the plane to the flight deck.

This work in a defense plant was considered top secret. Eloise explained they were told to say nothing about their work, not even to their parents. When I asked Eloise to describe her experience, she exclaimed, "It was the experience of our lifetime." I asked Eloise if she regretted any of her experience, and she replied, "Lord no, not a moment!"

Eloise married after the war and raised a family, and is now unfortunately widowed. She continues to lead an adventurous and independent life traveling around the country, visiting her old friends from the war.

As a modern child born in the 1980's, I didn't know exactly who "Rosie the Riveter" was. I had not understood the complexities and difficulties of these women seeking jobs in a man's world, nor did I understand really having to fight for freedom. Meeting an original Rosie the Riveter was no big deal until I truly comprehended the depth of her patriotism and bravery towards her cherished country.

"I Couldn't Jitterbug, ... So I Proposed."

by Jonnie M. Melillo Clasen
Columbus, Georgia
about her mother, Frankie Doris Thompson Melillo

Frankie and Vincent on their wedding day in 1945 (left), and a few months later, after Vincent was wounded

In 1945, Frankie Doris Thompson of Milan, Georgia was working in Macon, where she and Hazel Romans of Johnson City, Tennessee were managing the canteen at Camp Wheeler. The canteen was a place where soldiers could visit, dance, listen to music, and get something to eat. Frankie had graduated in 1943 from Milan High School, where she was class secretary and played on the girl's basketball team. Her cousin, Thelma Aides Fuller Linch, another Rosie the Riveter, lived in nearby Eatonton and worked for Enterprise Aluminum Company.

Called "Cissy" by her family, Frankie and her two older sisters were reared by their "Papa" after pneumonia killed their mother, the former Alice Cravey Walker, when Frankie was only 12 years old. Though resourceful, Frankie's rural roots didn't quite prepare her for life at Camp Wheeler. When Frankie was working in the canteen's snack bar one day, several soldiers ordered "pie a la mode." Frankie wasn't sure what the "a la mode" was, and another soldier in line, Vincent Melillo, told her it was ice cream. Vincent, born in 1918 to Italian immigrants in Boonton, New Jersey, was smitten with Frankie. "I noticed her the first time I went into the canteen," he said recently. "She was pretty and nice to people, and everyone liked her. I think she liked me right off the bat. I asked her for a date. Whenever I could get the company bicycle, I'd use it to court her. I serenaded her in English and Italian." The couple always sang to each other. Vincent was still singing to Frankie the day she died.

Frankie rented a room in a large old house on College Street. She was saving her money to attend business school in Knoxville, Tennessee, where her oldest sister, Mary Etta, lived with her husband, Tom McElroy. Her Papa was also living in Knoxville and working in Oak Ridge for the Manhattan Project, which developed the atomic bomb that brought WW II to an end. "We sat on the porch and visited," says Vincent. "Frankie was a great dancer, and everyone wanted to dance with her. I couldn't dance . . . well, I couldn't jitterbug . . . so I proposed to her." Frankie and Vincent were married at St. Joseph's Church in Macon on March 1, 1945. They spent their honeymoon on a 3-day pass at Indian Springs. Just months later, during a Camp Wheeler training exercise with live ammunition, a recruit hit a trip wire. Vincent was temporarily blinded, lost his hearing, and had his hand split open. The irony is that during WW II, Vincent had walked 800 miles through the mountains and jungles of China, Burma, and India as a Merrill's Marauder without getting wounded.

After recuperating in the hospital, Vincent received a medical discharge in August 1945. The couple moved to Knoxville, Tennessee where in June 1946, Frankie had a baby girl. Vincent, who had been working for Alcoa Aluminum, waived his disability in 1949, and reenlisted in the Army. He was soon reassigned to the Territory of Hawaii, where Frankie and his little daughter joined him until he shipped off to the Korean War in 1950. Vincent, a career soldier, and Frankie were married for 60 years before her death on November 9, 2005, at age 81. During their younger days, they traveled and lived throughout the world. They had two children, Jonnie Marie Melillo Clasen, and Vincent Franklin Melillo, who died at age 40 in 1997.

A Love Story

by

Alyson Miller Denyer
Rochester Hills, Michigan

*about her mother,
Dorothy Margaret
Smith Miller*

*Dorothy and Albert
on their wedding day, 1942*

My parents have been in love forever, you know, since they were a twinkle in God's eye, distant stars in heaven that fell to earth and planted themselves side by side in the West End of Pittsburgh, Pennsylvania, where they met when they were 16 and in high school. It was 1939 and war was on the horizon, but that didn't matter because Dorothy Smith and Albert Miller knew they were in love and never wanted to be apart.

They were nineteen when they married. On November 7, 1942, Father Erkin married them in the priest-house at St. James Church, where Dorothy went to school until the ninth grade. After the wedding, they whisked themselves onto the train to Akron, Ohio, and honeymooned in the tiny apartment Albert had been renting while working at Goodyear Corporation.

Dorothy got a job as a riveter in Firestone Park, not far from the apartment. Monday through Friday, she got up at

4:00 a.m., dressed in her dark blue overalls and sturdy shoes, tied a bandana on her head, and rode the 5:00 bus to the factory where she and other "Rosies" riveted parts for Douglas DC-3 airplanes. She didn't complain about cold mornings or hard work or wearing the same outfit every day, because it was exciting to be earning money and also fulfilling to toil on behalf of the war effort. Evenings and weekends were spent celebrating their marriage. She met many other women who were working as Rosies; they shared a common bond toiling together for such a worthwhile cause.

Albert was inducted into the Army in July 1943 and went to Fort Bragg for special training on 105mm Howitzers in the field artillery. Dorothy went to live with her mother in Pittsburgh. In September 1944, during her seventh month of pregnancy, her soldier boarded the *SS Aquatania* for Europe and his "tour de France." Their devotion flew on the wings of daily air mail – he cherished her every word; she cherished each tenderly written letter (and new French perfume!)

Dorothy had a little girl in October 1944. Albert was still overseas. The baby was named Alyson, to carry part of her father's name. Dorothy held her soldier in her heart until his safe return in January 1946, when he saw his daughter for the first time.

That's how love was during World War II. It was true and deep and everlasting. On November 7, 2007, my parents celebrated 65 years of marriage. God's eyes were twinkling again. And so were mine!

They have been in love forever, you know.

Dorothy and Albert at their granddaughter's wedding in 2006

My Trip Out West As a Pioneer of 1944

by Maebeth Mollberg
Dale, Texas

Left: Maebeth in San Diego, 1943, wearing the uniform issued by Consolidated Vultee Aircraft. Right: Maebeth in Texas, 2003.

My sailor was back from Pearl Harbor! I would take my 4-month-old baby, Amy, and myself to California to meet him, despite all the worries that my parents had about me traveling alone halfway across the country.

I could not wait, it had to be now! There was a train that made a direct connection from Austin, Texas to San Diego. All I had to do was have my Dad help me get on the train. Reluctantly, my Dad loaded the seat and overhead compartments and we headed west – just a modern Little Pioneer. Little did I realize what was ahead for us.

Finally we were in desert mountains near El Paso, when suddenly the train braked to a stop. Looking out the windows, I could see only the track perched on the side of the mountain. As we waited patiently, expecting to move soon, the conductor finally told us of a train wreck up ahead, and that we would have to wait until the tracks were clear! Getting outside was treacherous and inside was steaming. No air conditioning in those days! What a day that was with a cranky, hot baby.

At sundown we finally moved on. Then the conductor told me that because of the delay we would be going to Los Angeles instead of San Diego. Amy was going to be short of diapers, but thankfully had just enough milk. My biggest worry was how would I ever get us transferred to the San Diego train. At the last minute, a kind couple with two toddlers in tow helped me get into the train station, where I was stunned to see that the lobby was filled wall to wall with sailors and Marines.

When I found the right track, it looked like most of the men in the lobby were also planning to ride my train! A Marine standing nearby kept watching Amy. Finally, he came over and asked me if I was going to San Diego. He offered to carry Amy and I was to carry all of the luggage so we could get on the train early before the military. (In those days, the military families traveling together got on first.)

That Marine was a perfect gentleman. He held Amy all the way to Camp Pendleton, where he told me that the Marine base was his stop. I thanked him profusely for all of his help, and it was then that he confessed that if he had not been *so drunk* he would never have had enough nerve to hold a baby!

The rest of the trip was routine, and finally at San Diego, there was *my* sailor waiting for me! We collected our things, and needless to say he carried Amy so everyone could see that he was a new daddy, and I got to carry the luggage again!

Earlier during the war, I volunteered as a Candy Striper for the American Red Cross in local hospitals in Austin, Texas in 1943. After my marriage in June 1943, I worked in the Consolidated Vultee Aircraft Plant in San Diego, where B-24 bombers were assembled, as a clerk in an emergency rations shed. We packed emergency flares, food, parachutes, and other emergency rations to fly aboard the B-24s that were used as company planes flying between Consolidated quarters in Fort Worth, San Diego, Pearl Harbor, Midway, and Australia. We were provided uniforms, which consisted of the forerunner of pant suits! My salary was 80 cents per hour. I worked at Consolidated until my husband was shipped out to Pearl and I returned home to Texas in late fall of 1943.

Another Rosie for World War 2

by Jessie Belle "Jake" Moss
Cumming, Georgia

Paul and Jessie on their wedding day, December 30, 1942.

I'm from Cumming, Georgia, a small country town in north Georgia. I met my husband-to-be, Paul Moss, in 1941, the eve of World War II. He was from Alpharetta, a small town nearby. I was a long-distance telephone operator for Southern Bell in Atlanta, and Paul was in the U.S. Coast Guard aboard the Navy troop transport ship, the USS *Leonard Wood*. They carried troops across and brought the wounded back, as well as war prisoners. We married on December 30, 1942. We went to Norfolk, Virginia, where he was stationed, and I lived there while he made trips back and forth.

In August of 1943, Paul was sent to Honolulu, Hawaii

on the USS *Kukui*. I went back home to stay with my parents in Cumming. At this time they were calling for workers at the Bell Bomber Defense Plant in Marietta, Georgia, about 35 miles away, building B-29 Bombers. Wanting to do my part for the war effort, I went in training for three weeks as a riveter and in drilling. We were then sent into the plant where my crew was assigned to the fuselage department for fitting the skins to the frame of the fuselage, then drilling and riveting them on. I enjoyed the work very much and met lots of nice people.

Everything was top secret and we were checked coming and going. We had to go through long tunnels to get to our stations, and weren't allowed to take pictures inside the plant. I worked there for about nine months, until Paul got transferred to shore duty in Mobile, Alabama, where he worked at the USCG base in Civil Service until he retired in 1965.

While in Mobile, we raised our family of three children, Donna, Gary, and Mike. After retirement, we moved back to Georgia to be near family. I tell my grandchildren that I helped win the war by building the B-29 Bombers.

Paul and I have our names in the World War II Memorial Registry in Washington, D.C. for having served our country in battle and on the home front, and for this I am very proud.

To keep these WW II memories alive for future generations, my daughter, Donna, scrapbooked her father's military years from 1934-1947. With all the memorabilia we had saved, not to mention the 300 love letters, her scrapbook tells a love story that took place as World War II swept across Europe, and it would win a prize for authenticity and human interest of yet another story from the Greatest Generation.

My War Time Romances

by Mabel W. Myrick
Kimberly, Alabama

Mabel with Johnny Cisar,
June 16, 1944

My war time romances would very well parallel those of a young lady I heard about in the Pentagon. When she came to work with two bars pinned to her sweater, someone said to her, "I see your boyfriend is a Captain," to which she replied, "No, two Looies (Lieutenants)."

So it was with me. My first real love was during my senior year in high school, but he was called into service. I soon discovered he was not only writing to me almost daily, but to another girl in our small town. He sent me a cameo necklace from Italy – and the earrings to her.

A few months later, I graduated and went to work as a secretary in the Pentagon building. Washington was filled with service men coming through on their way to the war zones. There were also Navy, Army, and Marine bases nearby. Of course, this eased the pain of the first romance. We were still corresponding, but, as they say, "Everything is fair in love and war."

I soon met a soldier from Brooklyn. Johnny Cisar had been drafted – cutting short a promising baseball career with the Brooklyn Dodgers. We dated until the dreaded day he was deployed to the ETO (European Theater of Operations), when he gave me the ring he was wearing. We made a date to meet two years later on June 16, 1946 at the Plaza Fountain. After corresponding for several months, his family notified me that Johnny had been killed in Italy. I cared deeply for Johnny and the war was now getting too close to me.

I had dates with quite a few more service men. Then one evening, as some friends and I were dining out, I noticed two Lieutenants at a table nearby. One was especially handsome and I'm sure he knew he had caught my eye. He got up to make a phone call, the telephone booth being located right behind where I was sitting. He dialed several numbers without success and I could not resist telling him he had the wrong number. He asked for the right number. The next day, Gus called, then picked me up in a cab. We drove around to see the cherry blossoms at the Tidal Basin and had dinner. This began a romance that lasted two years.

When the war ended, I transferred to V.A. in D. C., where I worked for two years. I returned home at the end of 1947 and began to date my "first love" again, but the war had had its effect and things were not the same, and this romance ended.

Now, over 60 years later, I still have the cameo necklace, Gus's Lieutenant bar, and pictures and memories of Johnny Cisar and the date we could not keep on June 16, 1946.

My World War 2 Romance
by Margaret Neuhauer Nelsen
Cincinnati, Ohio

Robert and Margaret in 1941

    I met my future husband my first year of college at a Sunday night church youth supper meeting. For supper partners, we matched paper cutouts. I had the tail and he had the head of the same turkey.

    He had a pilot's license, and soon offered me a ride. From then we started seeing each other on campus. Soon it became steady. He was a good-looking, well-built, friendly, blond Scandinavian. Our backgrounds were alike. Our parents were farmers, and the Depression was on.

    I remember first meeting his parents. We hitch-hiked from Brookings, South Dakota, to South Sioux City, Nebraska. We enjoyed being together away from school.

    Then came World War II and my boyfriend enlisted in the Army Air Corps and was off to Flight Training School in California, where he got his wings and commission as 2nd Lieutenant. Before long he was in the European Theatre in England in the 313th Troop Carrier Group. During his years in the military, we met several times during his trips, transfers, or leave time.

My time as a "Rosie" was during Robert's time in England. I was graduated from South Dakota State University in the class of 1942. I taught school for one year, after which my best friend and college roommate was going to California to get married and then get a job. Did I wish to join her after her husband went overseas? I agreed and wound up at the Douglas Aircraft factory in Santa Monica, where I was a timekeeper in the machine shop.

The work day started at 7:00 a.m., and many weeks included Saturday and Sunday. Of course, I did not have a car and rode the bus to work. The contracts were "cost plus" on the plane being built then, which I think was an A-26. Every minute and hour worked by the machinist on each part had to be recorded. My job was to continuously collect the time slips and see that they were correct, and get them to where they needed to be. I hardly needed a degree to do that, but it made a man free to enlist in the service. It was a very simple and easy job, but I enjoyed it because I was moving about. I recognized workers who were, in large part, men who had not been drafted because of age, family size, or health. Many women and "4-F's" (men who did not pass the physical) kept the factories operating. 4-F was a classification that was not too popular because everyone really wanted to be in the military doing his part in that way. Patriotism was 100%. Rosies were actually riveting, doing a man's job and doing it well.

I did my little bit and enjoyed it, even when all car lights were on dim all the time, and street lights were shaded on the Pacific side. There was no way we were going to lose that war.

I stayed on the job until I got word that my fiancé Robert was seriously injured in action on D-Day, June 6, 1944. He was a C-47 pilot, dropping paratroopers over France. His plane was hit and he had a shattered femur. His co-pilot got the plane back to England, where he was hospitalized. He came to the States in a hospital ship in mid-October.

I quit my job and met him in Topeka, Kansas. We were married in the hospital chapel in Topeka on November 5, 1944. His left leg was still in a cast. Rehabilitation was in Santa Ana, California. He was then retired, and we were on our trip home to Nebraska when the war ended in Europe: V-E Day.

Moon Over the Palisades

by Opal Land Nelson
Cottage Grove, Oregon

Opal in the 1940's (left) with a sailor named Fuzzy, and more recently

The turmoil of a wartime world broke into our existence very seldom as we went about our daily lives. I was working as a riveter at Douglas Aircraft in Santa Monica, California on the graveyard shift. My roommate, Eunice, and I were totally involved in the war effort, though, for we went without sugar on our flakes, rode the bus to save gas, and made threats at Tokyo Joe like good patriots. We even found meat that didn't require a ration stamp – chicken gizzards – and we made many a soup from that delicacy. Otherwise, we didn't let the seriousness of the times interfere with our social schedule.

Our apartment in Santa Monica was our haven in a strange world. We had to keep our dating schedule straight. We had to be sure we didn't make a date with two different boys on the same night, and we had to be home by 10:00 p.m. in order to get to work by 11:00. Eunice and I tried to date only one branch of the service on a double date, since this eliminated awkward arguments. Dates waited on every corner.

But that was before Fuzzy! He walked into our apartment

and my life with a friend for Eunice one weekend, his Navy blue uniform accenting his boyish face. In the next few weeks, we danced at the Stage Door Canteen to Jimmy Dorsey, saw the New Year in at the Hollywood Palladium, and I wore my new dress with the pleats when we spent the whole day and evening on the Ocean Park Pier. His handsome face, with the dimple that twinkled when he talked, sent me skyward with dreams we didn't dare to dream in this uncertain world.

One Saturday afternoon, the Fuzzy that appeared at our door was graver, older, with clouded blue eyes. "I'm afraid this is it, honey," he said gravely. "Monday morning we ship out! Let's go for a walk in the Palisades." I reached for my sweater, though the evening was warm, as I felt cold. The laughter that usually accompanied our walks was gone. We had a feeling of foreboding. His hand was clammy in mine. I fought back the tears as we walked toward the sunset and talked softly of the good times of the past few weeks, not daring to think of the uncertainty of the next few. He would be heading for the South Pacific and the war had accelerated there. The day was ending except for the splendor of the remaining sunset. We stood very close and as the sky turned an indigo blue, we both felt it was a symbolic end to a beautiful romance, our hopes for a future dream, and maybe an end to life itself within numbered days.

With leaden steps, we turned to walk home through the park – and there it was! While we had been watching the darkening sky to the West, a gorgeous, big, mischievous moon had been rising through the palms and was lighting up the eastern sky with its glow. It lighted up our faces as if to say, "No, it isn't the end, just a bend in the road for a little while." We smiled at each other's tears, then we ran some, and laughed. Our farewell was sad, but full of hope and laughter and love and dreams.

Fuzzy did come back from the war, but we missed each other in the time warp that was WW II. I married and lived in Oregon. Many times since then, when the outlook is bleak, I turn and look at the promise of the moon. After my husband's death, I decided to look for Fuzzy on the Internet, and I put a personal ad in a Pennsylvania paper. I got a call from his daughter, who told me he had passed away several years ago. Strangely – and no one knew why – he had nicknamed one of his sons – Fuzzy!

Seeing the B-17, Then and Now

by Opal Breeding Nickell
Deland, Florida

Opal in 2007, standing next to a B-17 airplane like the ones she helped to build in the 1940's

I was a riveter on B-17 airplanes during World War II in Detroit, Michigan. I worked for Briggs Manufacturing.

We moved to Deland, Florida in 1973. The B-17's have been restored so they are flying to different states. People can see how they look and take a ride on them. One came to Deland in October 2007. My children took me out to the airport to see it. I took a ride and sat in all the seats – radio, bomber, co-pilot, gunner. It was very interesting. I never thought I would be riding in one that I worked on.

My son made pictures of the airplane. I bought a bomber jacket and joined the EAA. I get a magazine about six times a year and they are very interesting.

I have been a member of the American Rosie the Riveter Association for about ten years. I enjoy reading about all the happenings.

A restored B-17 plane that was available for viewing in Florida in 2007.

The B-17 flew in every World War II combat zone, but it is best known for daylight strategic bombing of German industrial targets.

Forever Young
by Hazel Young Parks
Toronto, Kansas

Hazel Young Parks

I was born Hazel Young in 1912; my parents were Thomas W. and Laura Young. I attended first grade in Kansas. I have a certificate from the school that states, "20 consecutive days without absence or tardiness merits this certificate." I had three sisters and two brothers: Howard, born in 1919, and Clarence, born in 1925.

I lived my early years in California. My father did dray work using horses and hayrack. We returned to Kansas and I married Arthur Parks in 1933. Our first farm was about five miles from Toronto, Kansas, but we farmed many years in Missouri. We purchased a farm in Kansas on our 14th anniversary. We farmed there for 23 years. We retired in Toronto in May 1970; I still live in our home.

During the war years, when Arthur got up early to do

farm chores, I called five or six women factory workers on the telephone to wake them up to insure they arrived to work on time. They did not have alarm clocks, and none were available for purchase.

I needed a washing machine. The store had one on display but none for purchase. I washed on the board, and I still have it. When rifles were available, I purchased one for Arthur and I still have it. I also have three oil lamps that are 17 inches high. One has a colorful bowl we purchased at a sale. One with a green colored bowl belonged to my grandmother, and a plain one is from the Parks family.

During the "poor drought years," Arthur did some road work, also. I had three surgeries and could not slop hogs and feed cattle. I worked in a café as cook, as the owner wanted "farm cooking." Other activities were needlework, singing, and church.

Arthur and Hazel. Note Hazel's needlework on the right.

When our First Christian Church celebrated 100 years in 2007, I sang my favorite song in the program. Our 50th wedding celebration in the American Legion hall included renewing our vows. The 5-tier cake had gold decorations – a fountain, doves, gold band rings, and "50." Our last anniversary was our 55th one.

Rosie the Riveter

by June Olander Pearce
Baton Rouge, Louisiana

June and Robert in Norman, Oklahoma, where they were married in November 1944

I was born and raised in Waukon, Iowa. My high school graduation took place in June 1940. Times were tough. If you had two nickels to rub together, you were lucky! After graduation I took a job at a local café. My work day was 14 hours for $1.00.

I remember Sunday, December 7, 1941 vividly. I had just met my girlfriends at the local café in town for a breakfast before church. All of a sudden we heard the café radio interrupt the regular programming with an emergency announcement. The Japanese had just bombed Pearl Harbor! How could this be? President Roosevelt made the Declaration of War the next day.

Our young men and boys rushed to the nearest recruiting office to sign up. My best friend, Eloise, had a letter from her brother in San Diego, California, that they were hiring women at Convair Aircraft. He had worked there about a year. Women in the factories were in high demand because the men were being drafted and trained for a long war. We said, let's go!

We had been working in the Ankeny Ordnance Plant at Des Moines, Iowa. This plant made cartridges for guns. We bought our train tickets and packed our bags to go out West. It was exciting and yet very scary – I had never been out of Iowa. After the cost of my ticket I had $60 left for this adventure, and I was 18 years old. I was truly a country hick. All of America was on the move to help win the war – everybody became transient.

Our trip took five days and nights on a coach car. There was no air conditioning – only windows to open. The desert heat just about finished us off – it was 120 degrees at night time. Cold wash cloths and kicking off our shoes and hanging our feet out the windows helped. When we arrived in San Diego, it was sunny and warm and I loved the adobe station with a red tile roof. Bougainvillea flowers were everywhere. This had to be paradise.

Eloise's brother met us at the station and said we could stay with him until we got a job and place to live. We were both hired at Convair. What a relief!!! We had six weeks of training, then they put us both to work riveting ribs to the outside skin of the plane. We hated the bucking rivet part, but got better each day. About two months later, they sent us to the main assembly line as electricians, to install wires in the planes sitting on a track. It was overwhelming to see all the huge planes (B-17 bombers) from one end of this gigantic hangar to the other. Our work day was 3:00 to 11:00 p.m. This was called the Swing Shift.

This is where I met my husband of 52 years. His name was Robert L. Pearce (Bob). He had a Southern drawl and a gorgeous smile. Bob was putting in the tail gunner wires. He also loved to dance and ice skate. After working all day, we would either go dancing at the YMCA or to the Ice Palace. Sometimes we would find a restaurant that stayed open late, and we loved the beach.

Before I started going steady with Bob, some of us would stop off at Pacific Square Ballroom. The service men needed a female in order to get in to dance. We decided to oblige because there were no strings attached. They had great bands – Woody Herman, Harry James, Ray Anthony, and more. If you wanted to jitterbug you had to go to a roped area to the side of the main floor. The boys were from all over. Very seldom did we see them again and I am sure some never came back from the war.

I left Convair to marry Bob, who had been drafted to serve in the Navy. I met him in Norman, Oklahoma, where he was stationed. Eloise and I traveled by Greyhound Bus because all the trains were being used for troop trains to transport the military. Bob was sent to Honolulu and I went home to help my folks on the farm. The war was finally over in 1945.

My Grandmother Is a Rosie

by Kenley Minchew
about her grandmother, June Olander Pearce
Baton Rouge, Louisiana

Fulfilling a dream

June Pierce of Baton Rouge stands in front of a B-17 on Thursday at the 8th Air Force Museum at Barksdale Air Force Base. Pierce traveled to the area to fulfill a dream of having her picture taken in front of one of the planes she may have helped build. "It was awesome," said Pierce of her experience building airplanes while working for the government during World War II.

Clipping from a Shreveport, Louisiana newspaper showing June in 2003. The caption reads, "June Pierce of Baton Rouge stands in front of a B-17 on Thursday at the 8th Air Force Museum at Barksdale Air Force Base. Pierce traveled to the area to fulfill a dream of having her picture taken in front of one of the planes she may have helped build. 'It was awesome,' said Pierce of her experience building airplanes while working for the government during World War II."

    As I reflect on my life, one particular person stands out among the rest. She is neither rich nor famous. She is a representative of ordinary women who have stepped in to accomplish "men's work" with little pay, respect, and recognition. My grandmother, June Pearce, or "June Bug" as I know her, is more than 80 years old and still going strong! June is an original "Rosie" and a member of the American Rosie the Riveter Association, ARRA.

June volunteered along with six million other women to work in an extraordinary workplace to support the men fighting for our freedom during World War II. The original "Rosies" not only gained tremendous respect, but opened many doors for working women today. Currently, the ARRA works to preserve loyalty, work ethics, and the history of working women. My grandmother gave her country everything she had to give: her money, her time, her service, and most of all, her loyalty, in an act of pride and love for the United States. It was widely believed that the wartime production was a miracle that could not have happened without the Rosies of America.

June's granddaughter, Kenley, a student at LSU

June has made an immeasurable impact on my life. The amazing motivation and passion she exudes for even the smallest task has encouraged me to strive for lofty goals. She has taught me that no matter how difficult a task may seem and no matter how many obstacles may stand in your way, success is bound to come as long as you continue to strive to achieve your goals. June has unintentionally altered my outlook on life and has made me a brighter person. Without her continuous encouragement and her strong-willed personality, I would not be the "Rosebud" she has influenced me to become.

Smile — We Did It!
by Nona Vanita McLemore Penner
Yukon, Oklahoma

Nona in the 1940's. The photo on the left was taken in a booth on the street in downtown Oklahoma City.

I was a farmer's daughter and grew up in the very small town of Colony, Oklahoma. Ours was a very small community, therefore many of us did many things to help with the war effort.

After school, I worked for the Red Cross, folding gauze into bandages. The Red Cross then sent them to military hospitals where needed. Many older women did this to help, too. To do this job I had to wear a hair net and apron and wash my hands with Lifebuoy soap. We also had to wear a top with long sleeves.

Food, gas, tires, and other things were rationed. We were issued stamps for all food, and clothing was limited. Everyone had gardens in their yards and by road sides. Everyone shared seeds, plants, and labor. My brother had been drafted into the U. S. Army.

As soon as I graduated from Colony High School, I traveled to Oklahoma City where I got a job at Douglas Aircraft as a riveter on a C-47 for a salary of 75 cents per hour. The nearest bus station was at Cobb Creek, five miles from my home, on Highway 41. The only bus line was Panhandle Transportation, and all the roads were dirt and sandy. My parents took me to the station to catch the bus.

My job was to rivet a piece of metal called the skin to a frame between the cockpit and the fuselage, which made the wall. I, the shooter, was on one side. My partner, the bucker, was on the other side. There were signals we had to use. When one of us made a mistake we would say, "We can do it!" and we smiled and did do it! We would work together to repair any mistake. We had a tool crib to check out rivets. I had a small canvas apron to store rivets and a special rack where I placed my rivet gun when not in use.

I lived in a basement apartment with my sister in Oklahoma City. I was in a car pool when I worked first shift, but when I worked swing shift (3:00 to 12:00), I rode the city bus. When we entered the plant gate, we women entered on one side and the men on the other side. We all had to open our lunch boxes to show our ID badges.

There was a Navy base in Norman. The Navy would send buses to Douglas, and on days we worked swing shift, we gals would go to the base and dance with the sailors until dawn. There were live bands and Big Band records on the nickelodeon. Navy buses would take us back to Douglas and then we would take city buses home.

On our days off, many of us would pack a lunch and ride the streetcar to Lake Overholster for a 10 cent ticket. A 25 cent token would take us to El Reno.

The day WW II ended, Douglas closed. I stood in line to check in my tools, then stood in another line for my final paycheck. There were celebrations, loud singing, and sad goodbyes. We DID it! Then unemployment awaited us at $18 a month.

Fiancé and Father Delay Wedding Four Years

by
Jonnie Melillo Clasen
about her friend,
Carlotta "Carrie"
de la Cruz Pettit
(an Allied Rosie who
served in England)
Columbus, Georgia

Carrie and Kevin celebrate on their voyage on board the Britannic *in 1959, when they emigrated to America.*

Carlotta "Carrie" de la Cruz's marriage was delayed four years until 1946, because it took that long to get her seaman fiancé, Kevin Pettit, and her seaman father, Domingo, home from their separate ships to Liverpool, England . . . at the same time.

"We decided to get married when we were 18, but we could never get the two of them together," says Carrie. "Every time Kevin came home from sea, my father was away and, well you see, he had to give me away at my wedding, didn't he.

"I left school when I was 15, and that's the year the war started," explains Carrie. She had already been working for a year in a factory when she met Kevin. "He was 16 too, but wanted to go away on the ships, so he told them he was 17 so they'd take him. He got a job as a stoker. The ships used coal, and he stoked the fires."

England had been at war since 1939, and Liverpool was being bombed on a nightly basis when the couple first met in a ballroom dance hall above Lee's Shoe Shop on Mill Street. "When the air raid sirens went off, we'd all go down into a shelter until the all clear. They bombed us during the night."

Rather than go underground into a shelter, Carrie's family chose to be evacuated outside Liverpool to Ormskirk where they "were billeted in an old barracks or school for the night." They were brought back into Liverpool each morning.

"I went a couple of times, but I was old enough to go underground into the air raid shelters, and I would hide sometimes so my mother couldn't find me. I wanted to be with the teenagers—not the old people—because there was singing and dancing underground. Fellows would play the accordion and guitar, and we enjoyed ourselves."

The first factory where Carrie worked was bombed, so at age 16, she went to work for an aircraft factory making racks that held bombs underneath airplanes. "I stayed there almost 2 years, and that factory got bombed, so I went to work in another factory making little fuses for engineers to use on ships. By then, Kevin was working on the newer ships, which had steam engines, and they used the little fuses I'd been making.

"We got married on a 48-hour special license because we didn't know when Kevin would have to go back to the ship. He got a new suit and I got a new costume. They were the same color—mariana blue.

"We finally got a flat in Caryl Gardens near the docks, which was lovely, because we'd never had an indoor bathroom. We thought we were 'posh.' All the relatives came to our flat to bathe. It was so different from war times because everyone was enjoying themselves. There were plenty of jobs everywhere. You could go to work and if you didn't like your job when lunch time came, you could quit and have a different job in the afternoon. It was an exciting time."

After Carrie's sister, Josephine, moved to America and was married, Carrie and Kevin followed, arriving in 1959. They settled in Union Beach, New Jersey. Both families eventually moved to Columbus, Georgia, where the two sisters remain following the deaths of their husbands.

With Western Union During World War 2
by Verlie Roberts Pope
Kimberly, Alabama

Verlie and friends, working at Western Union in the 1940's

During my last few years in high school, WW II was going on in both Europe and in the Pacific area, and by the time I graduated in 1943, I had two sisters and a brother working in defense plants.

My cousin was working at Western Union in Birmingham, Alabama, and she asked me to apply for a job there. When I went in for an interview, I was hired to go to work the next day. Western Union was located in the Peabody Building on First Avenue in Birmingham. There were three departments and I was hired for the Phone Department, working with a number of other girls on the switchboard.

This department was buzzing with the noise of people talking, typewriters, and the telefax machine. Not only did I work on the switchboard, but I typed lengthy government messages that were sent by tube to the Traffic Department on the second floor. The hardest part of this job were the government messages sent to families of service-related casualties, especially of those young men from my home town, one of which was my own first cousin. The casualty messages were delivered to the families by Motor Messengers, who were usually men who were too old to serve in the military. Messages not related to casualties were either delivered by telephone or, if local, boys on bicycles.

We had two breaks a day, 15 minutes in the morning and afternoon, and 30 minutes for lunch. We had a break room upstairs, but went out for lunch. My salary, after deductions, was $17 per week.

Since we shared the Peabody Building with several other companies, Western Union built their own building on 5th Avenue in Birmingham. While working at Western Union, I made many new friends with whom I have kept in touch throughout the years.

After the war was over, I met and married Howard Pope. I retired from Western Union in 1976 after almost 34 years. Howard and I were married for 41 years when he passed away in 1998.

In the Phone Department

How and Why I Became a Rosie

by Kathleen O. Powell
Loganville, Georgia

Kathleen in the 1940's

When I graduated in 1938 from the high school in Williamston, South Carolina, I was unable to attend college due to the illness of my mother. During September, I began working for the Town Clerk and Treasurer in the City Hall building. When Pearl Harbor was bombed by Japanese planes on December 7, 1941, World War II began.

Because the Town Clerk was a single man, he was soon drafted into the Armed Services. This meant that I was completing two jobs – mine and his. The office of the Town Clerk had always been a man's job, and if they replaced him, I would have to explain his duties to a new employee. The Mayor and the four aldermen decided for me to be the first female Town Clerk. Quite some time later, I was told that I was eligible to become a member of the American Rosie the Riveter Association because I had replaced a man who went into the Armed Services.

I wanted to be more active in the war effort, and in 1943, I became employed at a B-25 bomber air base near my home town. Because I had been experienced with finances, I was employed to be responsible for the reports of any business that worked on the base. And because this had been a man's job, I had again freed a man to be on active duty.

Many years later, during 2007, I was living near Atlanta in a retirement village, Southern Plantation. I attended a Rosie the Riveter national convention in Atlanta. When it was discovered that I had held two defense jobs during World War II, I was invited to become a member of the national organization.

At the present time, I am a member of a new Rosie chapter being organized in the city of Atlanta, and I look forward in the future to some new Rosie experiences.

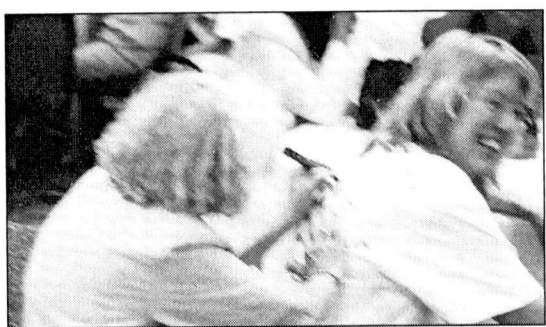

Kathleen autographs a T-shirt for Rosebud Donna Brockmann at the 2007 national convention of the American Rosie the Riveter Association in Atlanta, Georgia.

A Wise Mother

by Delores Price
Cincinnati, Ohio

Delores Price in July 2007

I indeed was a Rosie in the summer of 1943, when I became 16 years old. I was hired to sew tents for the military. It became a race to make as many tents a day as we could for our men in service. We recognized the officers' tents when they came to the conveyor belts. These had mosquito nets and doors and windows instead of flaps.

I was still a kid in high school and earned more than Mom, who supported us two kids. I thought I was as rich as Rockefeller, making more than Mom, and didn't want to go back to school in September that year.

Mom was very wise! She told me I couldn't live at home unless I went to school. I told her I'd move. Mom said I'd need furniture, and if I wanted a phone, lights, gas, refrigerator, radio, or anything else, I'd have to buy that, too. I soon got wise myself and decided to choose going back to school.

I enjoyed running the double needle sewing machine and putting the cut pattern of canvasses together to make great shelters for our troops. Bless 'em all!

Delores in 1988. Notice her motor home in the rear. Delores lived in her motor home after leaving Chicago where she had lived and worked. She spent time in Nevada, California, Arizona, or wherever. Delores says, "It's a great life!"

Twins at Boeing

by Wilma Mathauser Rees
Sun City, Arizona

Twin Rosies, Wilma Mathauser Rees (on the left) and Amelia Mathauser Kizer, in September 1942

It is September of 1942. My twin sister and I are working at Boeing Aircraft Company in Seattle, Washington. We are 19, from a small town in Nebraska, and are helping to build the B-17. This is a very special plane to us. Our only brother, who was in the Army Air Corps, had been lost on a B-17, flying on a special mission from Tampa, Florida to Miami. The plane and the crew of ten were never found.

There probably were more people working at Boeing than lived back in our home town. Boeing was a closed shop and we had to join the union in order to get a job. When the union couldn't get the benefits and raises they asked for, we union workers walked out on the job. It worked.

I was a rivet bucker. We put the skin on the end half of the wing of the B-17. The wing frame sat with the end pointing up and I climbed inside the frame The riveter inserted the metal pin and, with the rivet gun, drove it through a pre-drilled hole. I held an iron bar against it. Everything was inspected and if the end of the rivet wasn't tight and smooth, it had to be drilled out and replaced. We worked ten-hour days, six or seven days a week.

My sister worked in a different department, but we always went to the same rest room every day at the same time and got to see each other. Ladies would come by and say, "Are you twins?"

After a hard day's work, I usually fell asleep on the bus going home. It didn't matter whose shoulder my head rested on. People just smiled. They understood.

About a year later, my sister and her husband went back to Nebraska to help his father on the farm. They talked me into going back, too. I married a cowboy and lived on a Nebraska ranch, helping to raise cattle to feed the Army for the rest of World War II.

Twin Rosies Wilma (left) and Amelia in 2006 at their 65th high school class reunion

My World War 2 Story
by Donna Ruth Shrauger Roner
Salem, Oregon

Donna in Deer Park in the spring of 1946 (left) and in 1998

I graduated in May 1942 from high school at Deer Park, Washington. I worked for a while at the telephone company when it was "Number, please." I lived with a couple for room and board. I took their twin babies in the baby buggy out for walks.

Then I worked for a doctor and assisted in setting broken bones, being receptionist, etc., and I removed the tonsils of two patients.

I applied for a job at the aluminum rolling mill in Spokane Valley at Trentwood, Washington. I was called to come to work in January 1943. I moved to a room and boarding house that a lady named Mrs. Schalty ran. I had two friends living there.

I operated a lift truck first, moving scrap metal to the furnaces. This was mixed with a formula of various metals to make the aluminum for making airplanes. In a short while I was operating the crane (called "stiff leg"). We pulled the big slabs of metal out of the furnace, where they were heated for rolling out in sheets. We took the slab back to the rollers, laid it down, and returned for another one. Each operation took less than a minute. I worked with girls on the crane. The two operators rolling the slab (Ingot) out were one girl and one boy.

We worked 15-hour days part of the time. Our plant won awards for the greatest production. The slabs of metal weighed 1,080 pounds each, with a length of 108 inches, a width of 42 inches, and they were 6 inches thick, I believe.

For our work then, we earned just under $1.00 an hour. When V-J Day came, the plant was closed for a week, as I remember. Then we ran aluminum for car factories for a short time. Then the plant was closed, and there was no more work to be had.

I moved back to Deer Park. I worked in the coffee shop at the Deer Park Hotel. By June 1946 I had moved to Salem, Oregon, and I have lived here ever since.

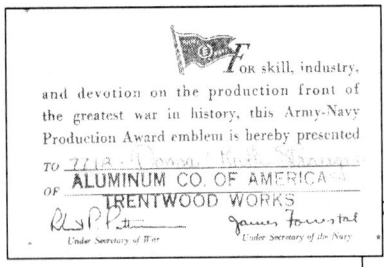

Production award presented to Donna while she was working at the aluminum rolling mill.

A Tale of Women in World War 2

by Drusilla Durham Methvin Rowe
Corvallis, Oregon

Drusilla in 1944 when she worked on the B-26 turret (left), and in 2008

In 1943, I responded to a Sun newspaper ad to take a three-month course in basic engineering at Johns Hopkins University, paid by Glenn L. Martin. After completing it, I took a four-month course in aeronautical engineering with 30 women. Among them was Violet Rinta, another Rosie. She and I remained dear friends until her death in 2006.

I worked as a junior draftsman on the B-26 turret until June 1945, when I married a young lieutenant in the Air Corps. His best friend, Harrison Jones, whom I planned to marry, died in the long battle for Casino, Italy. I joined Marc Rowe in Alamogordo, New Mexico in July. Six weeks later, the first atomic bomb was tested there, called

Trinity. Marc was on that field at 5:00 a.m., ready to fly, when he was grounded. He heard nothing, but it was as if the sun had risen to midday. I was 80 miles away in Las Cruces and heard a tremendous boom. Word was spread that the cause was an explosion of an ammunition dump. The truth was known when the war ended.

Marc and I returned to Baltimore to pursue civilian life. The Korean War in 1951 caused his recall to the Air Force, where we remained until his retirement. We raised five daughters while stationed at many great places: Fort Worth, Texas; Falls Church, Virginia; Colorado Springs, Colorado; and many lovely years on Oahu in Hawaii. While Col. Rowe retired on Oahu, I longed to return to the mainland, and chose a lovely college town, Corvallis, in Oregon. We returned in 1972. I now have two acres filled with flowers and many trees. Marc died in 1985.

Since we are honoring women who served in capacities in WW II, I thought I might add an addition to my tale. A random form letter from Meryl Streep alerted me to the fact that a group of women was trying to establish a museum on the mall in Washington, D. C. to honor many women in all walks of life who made important contributions. I therefore became a charter member in the National Women's History Museum, since my own great-grandmother was Dr. Cassandra Pickett Durham. She was the first woman doctor in the South, having graduated from Macon Medical College in 1870. At the end of the Civil War, she was left a widow with four children and a trunk full of Confederate currency. Relatives scraped up $200 in gold and enabled her to get her medical degree. The college and all records subsequently burned, and it was only in the past decade that she was honored by the state of Georgia. So all women, including Rosies, will finally get recognition in this museum.

Greetings and love to all of us Rosies whose lives were changed by WW II.

The Wartime Wedding of Erma Ellis and Bryce Scudder

by Kandis L. Scudder
Birmingham, Alabama
as told to her by her mother, Erma Ellis Scudder

Bryce and Erma Scudder on their wedding day in 1945 (left) and more recently

A boy by the name of Bryce, whom I dated, asked if I'd care to go to the school ball with him. I clearly recall that the gown was a filmy powder blue and I felt like I was floating on a cloud. During the evening, Bryce told us that he had enlisted in the Air Force and would be leaving December 15, 1943. That was just 12 days after his 19th birthday. It upset me. I had known him since I was in the fifth grade, but I was proud that he had the courage to enlist when he would have been safer on the family farm.

Our town was selected to be a plane-spotting station. I "enlisted" immediately. We were given detailed instructions and pictures of all German and Japanese aircraft to memorize, and a schedule was set up. Some planes were difficult to differentiate from ours, especially if they were a bit high for our high-powered binoculars. I reported several, but fortunately, they were ours.

After Bryce enlisted, letters began arriving from him, telling of the rigors of basic training and KP duty. After basic training, he was sent to Denver. Our letters began to take on a more serious tone. Furloughs of two weeks were cherished and were much too short. We discussed how foolish it was to marry while the war was still on.

One day, a letter came asking why we couldn't get engaged. I saw no reason why we couldn't, and let him know by return mail. A large box arrived a couple of months later and, after some digging, I found my diamond ring. I called him that night. We had become engaged via the U.S. mail and a long distance phone call. We were young and the war seemed endless. Finally, a letter arrived suggesting we get hitched on his next furlough. He had a talk with the Commanding Officer and was told he *wasn't* going to be sent overseas. We decided to get married.

In March of 1945 Bryce got a two-week furlough. We planned to have our wedding, but Bryce got a telegram ordering him to report back to base three days early. He shot a telegram back to a buddy. Kearns, Utah was the reply. This meant embarkation. We decided that we would go through with it. We would be married in my parents' home.

Bryce's brother was the Best Man and his sister was Maid of Honor. We had to walk down the "aisle" from the kitchen. Fortunately, the bathroom was off the kitchen, for I became sick. With my handsome soldier bridegroom waiting, I dashed into the bathroom and vomited. The pianist started "Here Comes the Bride" four times, and the fifth time, I made it. The Best Man broke the tension by rolling up Bryce's pant leg to his knee. He also rolled the opposite leg of *his* pants. Poor Bryce was so nervous, that he never knew this nut had done that! We heard the minister say, "I pronounce you man and wife" and the ordeal was over.

Our honeymoon consisted of one night in the Mark Twain Hotel in Elmira, New York. Bryce left Monday morning on the USS *Lurline* out of San Diego for Okinawa.

Not a Cigarette Between Us

by Ruth Slack Sedwick
Birmingham, Alabama

Ruth and Gib in 2005

A mutual friend introduced Gilbert and me. You have heard the saying, "love at first sight," but to me, it was more, "interested at first introduction."

Gib invited me to dinner and dancing. When he offered me a cigarette, I responded, "No thanks, I don't smoke." He didn't smoke, either. We dated for some time, and after Pearl Harbor, we were married on May 30, 1942.

He was soon assigned to training in California, but ended up in the Aleutian Islands with the Navy Seabees 4th Battalion. He returned home for a 30-day leave after one year.

After this, he was sent to Camp Parks, California, for further training. I had told him while he was home that I wanted to drive the new 1941 Chevy to wherever he was stationed in the United States. He telegrammed that he might be there for a while. I quit my good job at Curtiss-Wright Airplane Plant office, and headed west. A friend,

Esther, wanted to go, too, as her Army husband was in Oregon.

We left Columbus, Ohio, and crossed the Mississippi River into Kansas on old Route #40. We survived a tornado  ahead of us on the highway and arrived in Salt Lake City, where Esther caught the train for Oregon at 11:00 p.m. I stayed with her until she boarded, then decided to start west. The moon was shining like snow on the Great Salt Desert, and there was nothing on the highway but trucks. When I got sleepy, I pulled in back of a filling station until 6:00 a.m.

Before leaving Columbus, I had bought two recapped tires from a salesman who said they would take me to California. They did, but just across the line I had a flat. Just as I got out, a car from Ohio stopped behind me. Five uniformed Army fellows got out, and one changed the tire. I continued to Sacramento to spend the night with a girlfriend and her family. Next morning as I was leaving Sacramento, a city bus driver hit the trunk of the car. He failed to yield at a crosswalk.

I continued, and Gib was waiting. We had a glorious eight weeks there, then he was moved to Port Hueneme (California) before being shipped out on Christmas Day. Two other wives came back to Ohio with me. The round trip was about 7,000 miles.

We still did not smoke when, on May 30, 2007 we celebrated our 65th wedding anniversary. Gib passed away in January 2008.

Rosie the Riveter

by Darlene Crozier Semrad
Oklahoma City, Oklahoma

Darlene in 2006 (left) and in 2007 with other Rosies who attend her church

I went to work at Douglas Aircraft as soon as I finished college at Central State. I was privileged to work as a riveter for about a year, then the war was over and the plant closed.

I then taught school for a year before marrying Everett Semrad. We both went to O. U. and I received my Masters degree.

Several years later we had two wonderful daughters. After they were of school age, I started my career as a teacher and taught for 31 years before retiring.

At the time I was working, I lived in Edmond, Oklahoma. I now live in Oklahoma City, and have lived for 57 years in the same home.

I attend Asbury United Methodist Church. I am Chairman of my Sunday School class, a greeter for the church, and sometimes an usher. I am a historian for the church, a fill-in for the secretary, and some other duties.

I love sewing, cooking, and spending time with my two daughters, and I love my dog. I volunteered as a hospice worker, and for the Lyric Theater, the Science Center in Oklahoma City, and the Arthritis Foundation. I make cookies for the Ronald McDonald Home. I like keeping busy.

Included is a very important event that I want to mention. In my church, I got acquainted with a pilot of World War II. I found that he flew the C-47. On the next page is a first-hand report from him. The report shows how successful and thankful he was for our good work.

Left: Darlene in 2007.
Below: A certificate presented by the Oklahoma City Chapter of the American Rosie the Riveter Association.

And now . . .
a word of appreciation
from a fan . . .

The following letter is written to all who served as "Rosie the Riveter." It was passed along to us by Darlene Semrad of Oklahoma, who served as a Rosie.

> November 7, 2005
>
> Dear Ladies of "Rosie the Riveter" fame:
>
> What a name! But how appropriate a name. It could not better describe the jobs you did during World War II. Jobs that until then were for men only. Well, you proved otherwise. And without your service, the military services would have had a hard time getting enough men to fill the combat jobs.
>
> During World War II, I was in the Army, but after the war I wanted to fly, so I became an aviation cadet and got my wings at Vance Air Force Base. My first assignment was to Tinker Air Force Base, Oklahoma, where I became a C-47 pilot in November 1950.
>
> As you know, the C-47 was one of the aircraft that you produced at the Douglas plant on Tinker Field. And, as far as I am concerned, it is the most famous. I don't remember how many were produced, but they numbered in the thousands, and there are still some flying in this world.
>
> I must confess that I have had a love affair with the "Gooney Bird." I have flown about 10 different type aircraft but the C-47 is my favorite. The C-47 and I have flown from coast to coast, and from Minnesota to the tip of Texas. I have flown it to Panama, Colombia, Venezuela, Guatemala, Ecuador, Be-

lize, Costa Rica, Jamaica, and the Dominican Republic. I have flown it in good weather and in weather where one would say, "It's better to be on the ground wishing you were up in the air flying, than flying wishing you were on the ground having a cup of coffee." But the Gooney Bird always brought us back home. Oh yes, I forgot one place – Narsarssuak Air Base, Greenland. And on the Greenland ice cap, where our landing gear collapsed and we had to come back to the base by helicopter. Our poor bird is still up there, probably a few thousand feet below the surface. Oh well, you can't win them all. There was Mexico, too, and Curaçao.

Well, ladies, I wish to thank each one of you "Rosies" for the service you gave for our country. Having been a military career man of almost 28 years, I am sure that I have been not only on airplanes produced by you, but on Jeeps, trucks, ships, etc. You proved you could do a man's job, and did it well.

You deserve to be recognized on Veterans Day.

Sincerely yours,

Sam Asseo

SAM ASSEO
Lt. Col., USAF (Ret.)
C-47 Pilot

Thanks to the Rosies from *Captain Sam Asseo (on the right).*

Love Blooms for Doak Aircraft Rosie the Riveter

by Karen Hicks
Buena Park, California
about her mother, Emma Mummert Sewell

Marvin and Emma in the 1940's

Emma (Mummert) Sewell was born and raised in Mt. Carroll, Illinois. During World War II, she worked at the Savanna Army Depot where she boxed up ammunition for soldiers. Another female employee talked her into slipping their photos and addresses into one of the boxes, but they never really expected to hear back from anyone. Imagine Emma's surprise when she received a letter from a soldier who said he put her picture under his helmet every day for good luck. But the two never met, and fate guided Emma down a different path – headed towards sunny California where she would meet her future husband.

Emma always loved the sound of train whistles beckoning to her from a distance as she lay in bed at night dreaming of faraway places. As a young adult she acted on those dreams and moved to Torrance, California. She obtained employment as a riveter at the Doak Aircraft Company, and it was there she met Marvin Sewell, an easy-going guy with a big grin and a mischievous twinkle in his eye. Originally from Oklahoma, Marvin moved to California and found work in war production jobs after being denied into the military because of an old knee injury. With his wonderful sense of humor, there's no doubt he was attracted to Emma's contagious laughter. Perhaps he heard that laughter echoing throughout the Doak Aircraft plant on Emma's first day on the job, when her supervisor asked her to get a plane stretcher from the tool crib. Emma obediently headed off to retrieve this mysterious tool, but before she got too far, her boss chuckled and called out, "Wait, Emma, come back. There's no such thing as a plane stretcher." Emma burst out laughing.

Not only was Emma a good sport, she was also a beautiful woman with a radiant smile, and it didn't take long for Marvin to take notice of her. The first time they met, Emma was eating an apple in the Doak cafeteria. It was a relaxing retreat for the employees, and it had a jukebox stocked with songs by popular artists of that time. Maybe Guy Lombardo's "It's Love, Love, Love" was playing when Marvin walked in and saw "the most beautiful woman [he] ever laid eyes on." He meandered over to Emma's table and turned on the charm. "That's not much of a lunch," he said, referring to the apple. "How about I take you out for some bacon and eggs?" It was Marvin's favorite meal, which he enjoyed any time of day. After a little pursuing, Emma took him up on his offer, and soon she became the apple of Marvin's eye.

The couple married in 1948, had three children together, and celebrated their Golden Anniversary before Marvin passed away in 1999. Emma's memories have faded over the years due to Alzheimer's disease. But when asked if she remembered being a Rosie, she replied with enthusiasm, "You bet I do!" Her children and grandchildren certainly won't forget. After all, they wouldn't be here if Emma hadn't become a Rosie the Riveter at Doak Aircraft, where love blossomed between her and the co-worker with the warm, friendly smile, by the name of Marvin Sewell.

Rosie the Riveter

by Edna Agnes Jackson Siemens
North Richland Hills, Texas

Agnes in 1942 when she worked at Fisher Body Aircraft (left) and with her daughter, Linda Prindle (an ARRA Rosebud), at her 85th birthday party in 2008. Note the Rosie the Riveter birthday cake!

Memphis, Tennessee was never my permanent home, but that is where my story began. On April 21, 1923, Gilbert and Bertie Jackson became parents of their second child, named Edna Agnes Jackson. My weight was four pounds, but I probably had a loud cry for a tiny brunette.

Shortly after I arrived, Daddy realized his life-long dream by buying a 500-acre cotton farm in Tippah County, Mississippi, 60 miles east of Memphis. He moved his family there, where three more children would be born and educated at the local high school in Walnut, Mississippi. In April 1942 I graduated high school, being voted Miss Walnut High and the one most likely to succeed! I thought that meant working in a ladies' dress shop.

At that time, World War II was in high gear and that was the major concern of most of the men we knew. One day, when I was with some of my high school classmates, I was handed a folded paper that looked like a job application. The paper was for young women to report to Fisher Body Aircraft in Memphis, where help was needed to get fuselage parts ready for the planes going off to the war. I got my parents' permission, and off I went to Memphis where I would apply for the job.

After two weeks of training, a friend drove me to the gate of Fisher Body before 8:00 a.m. I was directed to the supervisor's office. He greeted me with a somber expression, knowing what I was facing – a life-changing experience. No one on our farm had to work without a day off, much less on Sundays.

I thought I was ready for the job after weeks of checking to be sure that the rivet had gone where it should be on the metal pieces that held the plane safely in the air. Why did the supervisor keep coming in to check on the young girls and their rivet guns? I thought I was doing a great job for our military men, who needed these planes.

Reversing my sleeping hours for doing the job wasn't going very well. One of my most frightful experiences was about to happen. I could not adjust to their schedule.

One night, I was in position to do the job, standing inches from the metal part that we were working on. I stood still, closed my eyes and stayed in the position to be working, but I was asleep standing up. Suddenly, I sensed that someone was standing behind me. There he was, a man in military uniform. Before I could say a word, he said, "Come with me upstairs, we have to talk. . ."

Then he explained what would happen when a plane got into the air with a rivet that had gone in wrong and caused a split by high winds. In a few minutes, we were going downstairs and I was sure he would fire me. But he said I was a valued employee to them because I had been trained, and if I was let go, they would have to train someone else to take my place. Enough said, I was wide awake and no more sleeping on the job. I had learned a valuable lesson. I was still working there when the need for those planes was not as urgent as when they had hired a cotton farmer's daughter.

I will never regret having joined other Rosie the Riveters in helping the U. S. in WW II. I am proud to be a Rosie!

A World War 2 Love Story

by Romaine Stone Smith
Garden Grove, Iowa

Bob and Romaine
in the 1940's

    I worked at Brewster Aircraft in Hatboro, Pennsylvania on fighter planes during 1943. One day a handsome man stopped by my plane and struck up a conversation with me. After many chats, he presented me with a little heart pendant that he said he made from the plexi-glass put in the plane windows. Then he asked if I'd like to go on a ride in one of the planes, since he was a test pilot. I eagerly said yes and looked forward to it.
    However, on the designated Sunday afternoon I waited and waited. He told me later that he came to our rooming house, but my older sister told him I wasn't home. She admitted it and said he was too old for me. I was eighteen. I never saw him again but I still have the heart.

Months later, on December 1, 1943, my sis and I were walking down the street in Philadelphia to catch a train to Hatboro where we lived. Among the hundreds of service men also walking around, two handsome sailors stopped us and started a conversation. They coaxed us not to go home but to go to the movies with them. Being fun-loving young teenagers, we accepted the invitation. We went out for ice cream (in December!), then to the movies. Several dates followed and that week my handsome sailor proposed and I said yes! He sent for me to come meet his family in Iowa, and I spent that Christmas on their farm.

Bob and Romaine in 1998

We celebrated our 63rd anniversary in June 2007. We have four children, two girls and two boys, ten grandchildren, and fifteen great-grandchildren.

We are still so much in love and are enjoying life to the fullest. I had a career in banking, and after Bob farmed for three years, he put in 30 years with Kenosha Auto Transport in Kenosha, Iowa, as an over-the-road truck driver.

We are back living in a small town in Iowa far from the hub-bub of the city.

Rosie the Riveter

by Emily Rice Spahn
Watonga, Oklahoma

Emily on her 87th birthday in December 2006

I worked in an aircraft plant in Washington state during World War II. My first husband, the late Raymond Rice, was a Staff Sergeant in the chemical department and was stationed in the U. S. Air Force at Paine Field at Everett, Washington, which is north of Seattle.

Since help was needed on the air base, I worked there from 1944 through the end of the war in 1945. My work was in the blueprint department in the hangar where planes were repaired. I found blueprints for the parts that aircraft mechanics were working on at the time. I was in the filing section, working with two other women, who were local housewives. The office was in an upstairs part of the big metal building where workers repaired or assembled airplanes.

There were lots of file cabinets and many blueprints, with an organized checkout system. Sometimes they would only look at the blueprints in the office and find what they needed to know. The pay was $45.13 twice a month.

I worked there until my husband was transferred to Ellensburg, Washington in early 1946, shortly before his discharge from the service.

In 1952, I married Freddie Spahn, who died in January 2000. He helped me raise my two young sons and was like a father to them. They are Darrell Rice of Watonga, a news coordinator at the *Watonga Republican* newspaper, and Wade Rice, who is owner of Blaine County Abstract Company with his wife, Debbie, of Watonga. Freddie and I were also the parents of one daughter, Celia, who is a financial consultant at Cornerstone Bank in Watonga.

I have four grandchildren, and I am very proud of all of them. Two of them are married and two are still in college. One is at Harvard in Boston in medical research. Except for the war years and later living a few years in Louisville, Kentucky, I have otherwise lived my life in Watonga. I worked for 12 years at the Montgomery Ward store here, and also later as an assistant to the coordinator of the Senior Citizens Center. I also kept up the card display for 16 years at Safeway/Homeland and what is now the present Karl's Apple Market. I remain active in the Watonga Senior Citizens Center, where I write a weekly news column and am a member of the Board. I was given a 25-year pin by RSVP in 2007 for my volunteer work over the years. I am a longtime active member of the local Lutheran church, where I have served as secretary of the Women's Missionary League for many years. I have supported and been a part of most events in Watonga.

At one of our recent Rosie meetings, representatives from the new building of the Oklahoma Historical Society borrowed an original picture I had brought, showing me receiving an award at Paine Field. They made a copy for filing in their historical accounts.

In 2004, the 29th annual Watonga Cheese Festival Parade set their theme as "Rosie the Riveter," a tribute to the efforts of women in the 1940's. Three local Rosies, including myself, were made parade marshals. We were each provided with a decorated golf cart to ride in, driven by our son or daughter. We felt quite honored.

A Rosie's World War 2 Travels

by
Laura B. Spriggs

Atlanta, Georgia

Sam and Laura with their daughter, Jean, in 1946

When I met Sam Spriggs for the first time in 1937 – he was 18 and I was 15 – I had no idea that our story would become a "wartime romance." We married on December 25, 1940, and lived and worked in rural Gwinnett County, Georgia. Times were hard, particularly for farmers, in those years, and I roomed in the nearest town and worked at the shoe factory to supplement our income.

When Sam joined the Army in late 1942, I made the momentous decision to travel with him to Battle Creek (Fort Custer), Michigan, while he was in basic training. I lived in a private home (turned rooming house) with other Army wives, and worked at the Kellogg plant, packaging K-rations. Sam came over to see me when work permitted, and we socialized with other members of Company B, 785th Military Police Battalion. My husband was so trustworthy and charming that other soldiers asked him to "squire" their wives to movies or restaurants with the rest of us, if they had to be on duty. We made wonderful friends then, including our landlords, the Ostranders, and Joe and Bea Whittington, who later lived in Warner Robins, Georgia, and remained our lifelong friends.

When basic training was over in April 1943, I moved again with B Company to Wilmington, California. There I soon began working in Wilmington Shipyards and became a welder after eight weeks of training. Apparently I demonstrated some good organizational skills, as I was soon promoted to the office, doing production reports. I have a memory of the manager singing "There She Is, Miss America" when I walked into the office, behavior that would definitely not be tolerated in today's workplace!

After a few months, the Company was sent to Camp Anza, many miles inland from Wilmington, for further training. In a particularly memorable and romantic act, Sam got together a group of soldiers to drive back to Wilmington on the weekend. Several wives were watching a documentary about Adolf Hitler and looked up to see these handsome Army guys walk in!

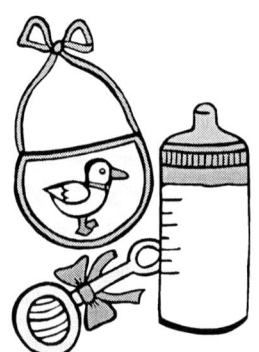

The wives and soldiers went back to Fort Custer in March 1944. Then the day we had always dreaded came – they left for Europe on September 5, 1944. But Sam and I had a suspicion that I was pregnant when he left, which was confirmed when I returned to Georgia. On April 22, 1945, we sent news to Germany that our daughter Jean had been born. Eight months later, my soldier returned to Georgia from the European and Pacific theatres of war, much to the amazement of our daughter, who wondered why there was a stranger in our bedroom! This wartime romance ended happily, and we were married for 49 years.

I Want to Marry That Girl

by
Clarentine Blasi Tasset

Pratt, Kansas

Claud and Clarentine on their wedding day, October 22, 1946

During World War II, I was one of thousands of women who worked as a riveter in an airplane factory in Wichita, Kansas. Near the end of the war, I went to Cosmetology School, and after graduating, I began working in a beauty shop in the small town of Pratt, Kansas. Meanwhile, Claud Tasset served his country in the Navy, and following the war, he moved to Pratt and worked for his brother. One day, I went to a dance with some friends in Kingman, a small town close to Pratt, met Claud, and we talked and danced together several times.

A few weeks later, Claud saw me coming out of the Sacred Heart Church in Pratt, turned to his sister who was with him and said, "I want to marry that girl." Claud had learned that I worked in a beauty shop in Pratt when we talked at the dance, so he asked his sister to help him find the girl he wanted to marry. His sister called all the beauty shops in Pratt, looking for a blond hairdresser named Clarentine. When she found me, Claud's sister asked me if I would speak to her brother.

Claud and I had our first official date on July 4, 1946. We were engaged one month later and were married on October 22, 1946 in St. Leo, Kansas. We remained in Pratt. I ran a beauty shop in our home and Claud owned The Pratt Monument Company before he sold it in 1981.

We have four children and eight grandchildren. Claud is retired, and I play bridge and still work as a hairdresser in our home. We celebrated our 60th wedding anniversary on October 22, 2006.

Claud and Clarentine on their 50th anniversary in 1996

Rosie the Riveter

by Betty Tucker Taylor
Orange Beach, Alabama

Betty at age 18 in 1944

World War II was raging when I graduated from high school during 1943 in Lineville, Alabama. My mother, sister, and I made the momentous decision to leave Lineville.

We packed our belongings and went to Heflin, Alabama, to catch the train to Savannah, Georgia. We pulled into the big station in Savannah and I was so awed by the station and all the mass of people coming and going, that I was ready to catch the next train back to the homey confines of Lineville.

Housing was scarce in wartime Savannah but we found an apartment. The next order of business was to apply for jobs at Southeastern Shipyard. We were sent to welders' school and graduated in six weeks as first class welders, at a pay rate of $1.20 per hour. Our first assignment was working in the yards welding on Liberty Ship parts.

They asked for volunteers to go up on the ways and weld, so I volunteered. My job was to weld on the overhead and the innerbottom in the Liberty Ship itself. We were required to keep a bandana on our hair at all times. My welding equipment had to be adjusted by a machine down on the ground. In order to do that, you had to climb down and back up a ladder on the side of the ship. If you did not get it adjusted right, you had to go all the way back down again. One day, I almost lost my fingers while leaning over the side of the ship looking for the machine. A whole bulkhead being put down by a crane came down right where my fingers were.

There was another close call when I stepped on a loose board and almost fell down the hole of the ship. Some men grabbed me and kept me from falling to the bottom of the ship. Several people were killed and others were seriously injured due to mishaps. I decided to quit several times, and finally went to the office and told them I wanted to quit. They told me that I could not quit, as this was an essential defense job.

The ship was not complete when launched. It was taken to wet dock for finishing. I helped launch a ship and watched it slide down the ways. They would let women watch, but you better not get on the ship when it was launched, as it was considered bad luck.

We would go home at night after work and grate potatoes to put on our eyes to draw the burn out caused by welding. My sister and I would take a shower and go out with friends. Our dates were boys in the Army Air Corps at nearby Hunter Field. It was always night when they left in their planes for overseas duty. They would fly low over our apartment and rev their engines to tell us goodbye. We never saw them again.

As things wound down during 1945, we were given our releases. Those were certainly exciting times!

Courting In the Olden Days

by
Carrie Hill Thomas

Tuttle, Oklahoma

Carrie at an ARRA chapter meeting in 2006 with her Rosebud, Paula Burgess-Cook

Over 70 years ago, two young men were living on farms near Newcastle, Oklahoma (about 20 miles from Oklahoma City). My family lived on a farm near Bridge Creek (7 miles west of Newcastle). In those days, there were few cars; most people walked or rode a horse to where they wanted to go. One of these young men, Melvin "Choc" Chrisman, was dating my sister, Pauline Hill. Choc did not own a car, but his friend, Rullon Thomas, owned a pickup. Choc talked me into going on a blind date with Rullon. All four of us crowded into the cab of the pickup and went to a country dance. It was not unusual for young people to walk four or five miles to a party or dance. We four dated together for several months.

Rullon had another friend, Jack Davis, who wanted to date Rowena Petty, a friend of mine. Rullon and I got them together, and the four of us dated for a while. One day, we decided to all get married. Since it was during the Great Depression and money was scarce, we had a double wedding in front of a Justice of the Peace in Oklahoma City on February 25, 1937. I was 19 and Rullon was 23.

When a couple got married in those days, their friends always gave them a shivaree on their wedding night. Friends would wait until around midnight, and come to the newlyweds' house and make all the noise it was possible to make. We told our friends to come early and we would have a dance. They arrived with cow bells ringing, horns honking, and pots and pans banging together. We invited them in and had a great shivaree wedding dance.

Rullon's mother had an old vacant house on her farm. The four of us had spent several hours cleaning it up and getting it ready for the dance. We spread cornmeal on the rough wood floor to make us "glide" as we were dancing. We gave candy to all the women and cigars to all the men. Neither my dad nor Rullon's mother approved of dancing, but they went along with our plans and didn't raise a fuss. We had a wonderful time dancing past midnight.

Rullon and I had two children, Joyce and Bud, and we were married for 69 years. When the children were small, I worked as Rosie the Riveter for two years during World War II. I worked on C-47 airplanes at Douglas Aircraft. I really felt I was helping the boys to come home.

Rullon and Jack are now deceased, but Rowena and I are still hanging on. I still do my own cooking and cleaning, and am able to keep up my flower beds. My son Bud mows my lawn, and his wife, Diana, does most of my grocery shopping. She also is great at keeping my sewing machine working smoothly and threading needles. Thankfully, I am still able to live in my own home.

Carrie (front row, center) with others at a recent Oklahoma ARRA state meeting.

The Behind-the-Heroes Scenes
by Allie Mae Thompson
Sun City West, Arizona

Allie Mae in 2008, on her way to the monthly meeting of her chapter of the American Rosie the Riveter Association

It was World War II and many of the men were called off to war. The United States had saved scrap metal for Japan for years, but when the Japanese bombed Pearl Harbor on December 7, 1941, it was time to stop saving scrap metal and defend our country. I loved my country and I wanted to do something for it. I left home and went to Richmond, California, where I got a job in the Kaiser Shipyard as a welder. I took my two children, a baby girl and a small boy, one year old.

I had to wear a leather suit with a hood with a window so I could see what I was doing. We used welding rods. Sometimes while I was working, a small spark or small piece of slag would land on top of my shoe.

I never imagined that I would see movie stars in person, but sometimes at lunch different stars would perform on stage for us – Bob Hope, Roy Rogers, Dale Evans, and others. Of all the different stars, I liked Bob Hope the best.

One day while I was working, another lady grabbed my electric lead line. I told her she should get another lead line, and that the one she had in her hand was the one I was using.  She didn't let go of the lead line. I took one look at her face and her eyes, and I got scared. Of course, I let her have the lead line. My supervisor found me another lead line and a different place to work.

The military needed many things that the civilians also needed. We were given ration books with stamps in them that were used to buy food, gas, tires for cars, shoes, and so many other things. If you didn't have the right stamp, you didn't get the item you wanted. My sister Velma and I couldn't get stockings, so we painted our legs with liquid powder and drew a dark line down the back of our legs so it looked like we had stockings on. Some people planted Victory Gardens so they could have fresh vegetables.

In 1944, there was a blast in Port Chicago, California, the largest state disaster during the war, killing 320 people. God was with Velma, as she was visiting our parents. When she heard about the blast, Velma told Dad that she had to go home. Dad told her that she might not have a home to go to, that he had been listening to the radio. Some employees had not been instructed as to how to do a certain job, and whatever they did caused a horrible blast. The town of Port Chicago was almost destroyed. The employees who were not killed were transferred to the Kaiser shipyard in Richmond, and some distance around the bay to another Kaiser shipyard.

Our Rosie and Rosebud Story

by Rena Coleman
about her mother, Allie Mae Thompson
Sun City West, Arizona

Rosebud Rena Coleman and Uncle Sam ringing a replica of the Liberty Bell at a Fourth of July celebration in 2007

I am not one of the Rosie the Riveter ladies, but I honor and respect them all for helping win the war. My mother, Allie Mae Thompson, was a Rosie the Riveter, so that makes me a Rosebud in the American Rosie the Riveter Association. Here in Sun City, we have a club (chapter) that meets once a month. We have lunch and talk about the jobs that each Rosie did during the war. I think a lot of people don't know about these wonderful, hidden heroes. They should be honored and never be forgotten.

My mother was a welder. I was one year old when my mom left home, taking me with her. She went to Richmond, California and got a job as a welder in the shipyard. She has told me about the funny leather suit and the hood for her head that had a glass in it so she could see. She told me about the movie stars who would perform for the workers, and how much the employees enjoyed the performances. Sometimes when she is talking about her experiences, I wish I could have been able to watch her while she was doing those things.

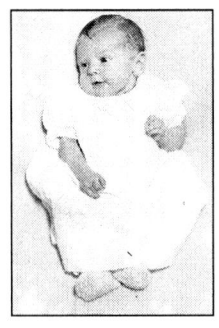

We lived with my aunt and uncle, and they took turns taking me to the nursery. My mom says that she was very happy to be able to do something that would help win the war.

The military needed many things that the people at home needed. The people at home were issued ration books with stamps in them that they could use to buy things they needed. If they didn't have the stamp, they didn't get the item they wanted. Mom was happy to do things. We love our country, and we were proud to have won the victory of the war. My two grandfathers, two grandmothers, my Aunt Velma, and my uncle worked in the Kaiser shipyard. My two uncles were in the overseas battles, and one worked at a medical place.

Mom says that when the war was over, the people in New York were throwing shredded paper out of the windows, and some people were dancing in the streets. They were so happy the United States had won the victory.

Billy and June Tinker,
on their wedding day in 1953

My Second Husband Was My Savior

by
Jonnie Melillo Clasen

about her friend,
June Midkiff Tinker

Columbus, Georgia

    The letters "about everyday things" that June Midkiff wrote to two soldiers in two separate wars resulted in two marriage proposals, two very different husbands, and two extremely different lifestyles.

    June was a "starry-eyed" 16-year-old teenager in 1941 when she was "swept off her feet" by a much older man named Tom, who was 20, at Edwight Mine's company town, where they both lived on the Big Coal River in West Virginia. "Both our fathers were coal miners," says June. "We lived in company houses and didn't have any indoor plumbing. There was a water pump at so many intervals on the block, and Tom lived near the corner where I had to go get water. He would come out and talk to me, and I thought he was so handsome. He had black hair, a mustache, and a real deep voice. I wasn't allowed to date. We didn't go anywhere. We used to walk up and down the road holding hands or we'd sit on the porch and talk. I fell in love.

    "Then Tom joined the Army and went away, but we kept in touch with letters. After about a year, I quit school and joined the National Youth Administration. I went to Charleston for three months and trained to be a welder.

"I was 17 years old and my sister, Hope, was 18. We went to work at Patterson Airfield in Fairfield, Ohio, which was near Dayton. I worked as a riveter on B-25's and B-29's, and as a sheet metal worker and in blueprinting.

"The horror of the war was very real when we saw how shot up the B-29's were that were sent back from the war for us to repair. I had two brothers in the Marines. Kenneth was killed at Iwo Jima. Jake suffered from shrapnel wounds all his life.

"Tom and I kept writing, and he proposed in a letter. After his medical discharge, we were married. We got an apartment in Springfield, Ohio, where I continued to work at Patterson Airfield. After I had gotten pregnant, he came home one day and said he'd joined the Merchant Marines and would be leaving. I went home to West Virginia. I didn't hear from him until after our baby girl, Deanna, was born. He hadn't joined the Merchant Marines. We never did get back together.

"I met my second husband through letters. My brother-in-law, Brace Wright, who was my sister Hope's husband, was serving in the Korean war and told one of his buddies, Billy Tinker, about me. He said I'd been married, was divorced, and had a 10-year-old daughter. I guess we'd been writing eight or nine months when he came to meet me and we just clicked off real good. He said, 'I guess you know that before I leave, I'm going to ask you to marry me. I fell in love with your letters, and now that I've met you, I know I want to marry you.' We were married when he returned to the States in 1953.

"I had 26 years of marriage and two children, Billy and our daughter Tiny, with Bill Tinker. He adopted Deanna and cared for her just like he did the others. He died in 1980 with a service-connected disability.

"He was 30 when he got married, and family came first with him. He knew that I'd had a pretty rough time raising a child by myself, and he wanted to take care of me. I loved his caring ways. My second husband was my savior."

June is spending her "golden years" as a singer, songwriter, musician, and yodeler. She was also Ms. Senior Columbus Georgia in 2005.

A Commemorative Remembrance

by Nancy Treu Klotz
Atlanta, Georgia
about her mother, Bertha T. Treu

Bertha Treu on her 95th birthday, September 16, 2000

The memory of my mother, Bertha T. Treu, during World War II was of a wonderful person who never complained about the war and all our efforts to win, which required sacrifice from everyone. She went ahead and did her part for A. O. Smith, a big company on 27th Street in Milwaukee, Wisconsin. The company manufactured articles for defense, and someone had to keep the books on what was spent for the war effort. She and my dad discussed the matter of working for the company on the night shift. The pay was more, and my dad agreed to take care of me with the help of my grandparents, who lived downstairs.

My grandmother did the cooking, but I missed my mother at mealtime and bedtime every night. After supper, I had the attention of my dad all to myself. We faced the blackouts the city would have, and wondered how my mother felt, going through the same thing.

On weekends we were all together and called upon my other grandmother for Sunday night supper, which she prepared for us and my dad's two brothers. My mother and I would go to a movie on Sundays, too. Sometimes in the warmer weather we would all walk to Washington Park nine blocks away, all holding hands. My mother and father were not the ones to demonstrate a lot of romance in public; yet I knew they loved each other by the way they treated each other and me.

My mother would help the neighbors out with sugar, coffee, and other staples. I was an only child and their stamp rations would deplete faster, so my mother would bake her "economy cake" (much less sugar, butter, etc.) and give it to the neighbors with more children. They devoured it with gusto.

At Christmas time, my mother made sure everyone she knew got a present of some kind. She was not a person who sewed gifts, but she made sure there was a little something for everyone, somehow. I still have a few of those things around that people gave back to me when my mother died on March 1, 2002. One thing I will always remember is her acceptance of whatever she had to face, and doing it with respect and dignity. Thanks for the memories!

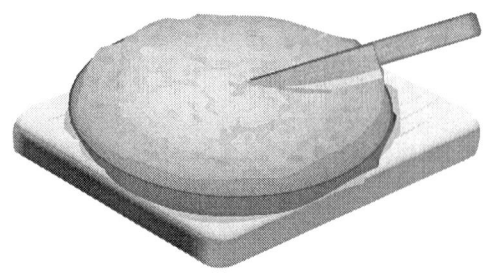

World War 2
Home Front Memories

by Lucretia Jane Tucker
Rome, Georgia

Jane at age 17 in 1944

World War II followed close on the heels of The Great Depression. In fact, very little recovery had taken place in my hometown, Lineville, Alabama, when the war began in 1941.

My mother, like most people during the 1930's, had struggled to support her family. So when news came from our cousin in Savannah, Georgia, that women were being hired to replace men in the work force, we were on our way to becoming "Rosies."

In June 1943, my mother, my sister, and I boarded the train to Savannah. Every seat was taken by the troops. Seeing this large number of men (boys 17-19 years old) leaving home for the battlefield made us know the war was real. Our luggage became our seats for the 15-hour trip.

Two weeks after arriving in Savannah, we were employed as welders at Southeastern Shipyard. I remember how shocked I was to learn that the hourly wage was $1.20. To a 16-year-old who had been earning $1.00 per day in the Lineville 5 & 10 cent store, this was unbelievable.

I recall the feeling of being shunned by "the locals." For women to take a man's job, even though the men were gone to fight, was not acceptable to many of the people. The general idea was that women weren't strong enough physically, and that women should not wear men's clothing. Well, we just rolled up our shirt sleeves, tied up our long hair with a bandana, and said, "We can do it."

As a teenager, I learned some valuable lessons. The U. S. government needed money for war supplies, and everyone was encouraged to buy War Bonds. Every pay check, I purchased a War Bond. An $18.75 bond matured to $25 in ten years. When I returned to high school and college, these bonds helped with expenses.

A second lesson came from having contact with people from many different states. Living in Alabama during the 1930's, I had never known a person from "the North." In Savannah, our social life revolved around the military bases, Hunter Air Base and Fort Stewart. Doing our patriotic duty – keeping the troops entertained – introduced me to boys from many states. These boys were friendly, kind, and treated us like ladies in every way.

Recently, I read the following quote posted in the Rosie the Riveter World War II/Home Front National Historical Park in Richmond, California:

You must tell your children, putting modesty aside, that without women, there would have been no Spring in 1945.

I am overcome with awe by this statement. As a 16-year-old, I could never have imagined that the 10 hours per day, 6 days per week of hard work was this important. How thankful I am that God allowed me to be a part of this fight for freedom.

Keeping the Troops Rolling

by
Marjorie Backlin
Van Alstine

Lacey, Washington

Marjorie Van Alstine

Yippee! Graduation 1943, and I can leave this valley in Montana, where I have been raised, and see the world. First stop was Vancouver, Washington, where I worked in a cafeteria, feeding shipyard workers. There I met a girl from Montana who became my friend, roommate, and travel partner.

In the fall of 1943, we left for Seattle, and worked at Boeing Aircraft, Renton plant, as riveters. Two of us replaced rivets that were not acceptable. These were kept on dry ice until warmed by riveting on them. One day I went to the tool room for a fresh supply. My fellow worker reminded me to take the metal container for them. But instead I put them in my shirt pocket. What a mistake! That took much of the cockiness out of 19-year-old me.

On the next page is a copy of my Boeing pass. I changed my age on it so I could enter the nightclubs so popular at that time. But I met no one there like my memory of the handsome 16-year-old Montana cowboy I first met when I was 10 years old.

After one visit home, we moved on. Our next stop was San Francisco to work at Kaiser Shipyard #4 in Richmond, California. We were apprentice Joiners, installing soap and toothbrush holders, shelves, and towel bars in the bathrooms (called Heads), and grab bars for hallways, etc. in ships. Several in our gang installed locks and keys. Once we locked ourselves in a stateroom for a party. The only thing "edible" was a tobacco plug, so we all took a chew. My, what a sick bunch left that room!

My Montana friend joined the Marines. One of the ladies in my gang invited me to live with her and her family. (Later I found out that this lady was a kleptomaniac and her husband was a wino.) Their 12-year-old daughter and I celebrated being "teens" together and it was said that I was like "one of the family."

V-J Day was past and soon the war would be over, so I went to work at Mare Island, a permanent shipyard. Later, I returned to Montana where I married that tall, handsome cowboy.

My war work was challenging, earning sufficient pay for treats like footlong hot dogs. But the greatest part of my life was to come!

After my four children were grown and my second husband died, I asked Jesus Christ to be my guide. He gave me four wonderful years as secretary in Hong Kong for Youth for Christ and Training Evangelistic Leadership. I have now seen the world in China, Singapore, Philippines, India, Israel, and Cuba, but the good old USA is the best!

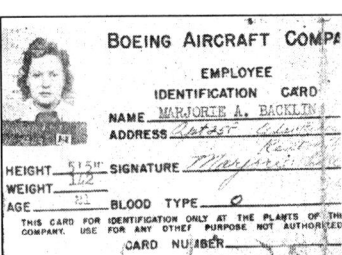

Marjorie's work pass while at Boeing

Memorable World War 2 Occurrences

by Nelle Eatherton Waldroff
Portland, Oregon

Nelle in her welding gear in the 1940's (left) and in 2006

In 1944, while I was working as an acetylene pipe welder at Oregon shipyards in Portland, I had a very narrow escape with my life. One of the welds was around a valve in the bottom of the 30-foot deep settling tank on the Liberty Ship that was used to warm the crude oil. The only exit was up a 30-foot ladder that was about 18 inches wide and went to the deck at an access hatch.

During lunch hour on the graveyard shift, the air blowers were turned off. I didn't notice they had not turned on, and started welding. I got dizzy and immediately turned off the torch. I couldn't hear the air blower and knew I had to get out, as I had used all the oxygen. I got up the ladder and passed out on the deck.

The medics were called, and I went by ambulance to the nearest hospital, where I was in an oxygen tent for two days. I went back to work a week later, but was always sure the air was on. I'm sure that incident, plus welding galvanized pipe, is what is causing my breathing problems at 82 years of age.

Another close encounter came not too much later. I had trained at Vocational School and had passed tests on both acetylene and arc welding, but since "gas welders," as they were called, were fewer, that was the job I obtained. We were making 72 ½ cents an hour, good money for the time, but certified welders made more, and I wanted to be able to say I was a certified welder.

The test was really difficult – a 6-inch piece of pipe, beveled at two places with a piece of iron behind. It would take five complete welds to fill the bevel. Needless to say, you had to use the largest tip to maintain enough heat to complete the weld to pass the breakage test.

I burned the knuckle on my point finger on my right hand, and got blood poisoning in the sore. I kept trying to work, but one night I had to give up and go to Emergency. The only thing they could do was keep packs on it, as the streaks were up my arm by the time they got me settled. Sulfa and penicillin were only for Army use, so I was in the hospital a week before the danger was over. Civilians didn't get Purple Hearts, and my injuries were nowhere near what our fellows were going through, but I did give my best for the war effort.

The caption for this newspaper picture read: "Reports of heavy invasion casualties brought a noticeable increase in yard blood donations. Above are members of the Pipe department graveyard shift ready for an early morning trip to the blood bank." Nelle is third from the right on the front.

My Rosie the Riveter Account

by Joyce Jaynes
Jonesboro, Arkansas
as told to her by her mother,
Lillian Beatrice Sanderson Walker

Lillian in the 1940's

I was 21 years old and I rode a train from Dennis, Mississippi by myself out to California to the Richmond (Kaiser) Shipyard. It was the first time I had been away from home.

It took about five or six days to get to California. The train was loaded with draftees and soldiers going out to California to be shipped out overseas. I had to sleep sitting in my seat, because the sleeping berths were reserved for the soldier boys.

As soon as I reached California, I attended two weeks of welding school. I started out as a tacker. That meant I would weld small spots to hold just until the main welder could get to it. We built some of the bigger ships for carrying troops, and we built corvettes, which were smaller ships that carried ammunition. They were very fast ships.

I worked outside on the deck of the ship. We could look straight across the water from where we were working  and see the Golden Gate Bridge. I arrived at the beginning of the war and tensions were high. Sometimes we would look out at the ocean and wonder if we were going to be bombed. One morning when I was going to catch the bus to go to work, the air raid sirens went off. It seemed as if every step I took, the siren got louder. The next day they told us that Japanese planes had been sighted 400 miles off the coast.

There were enjoyable times, too. Every day at lunch, the company would bring in some kind of entertainment. Once, the Andrews Sisters came. We worked six days a week. My husband, Rufus Walker, also worked at the shipyard as an electrician. He joined the Merchant Marines close to the end of the war.

The pay was good for the workers. In Mississippi, I had gotten a job through the WPA doing housekeeping and making $26 a month. Sometimes I would stand and iron all day. Working in the shipyard, I made $60 a week. I saved enough during the time I worked there to buy my mother a house, back in Mississippi. My younger brother and sister still lived with her. I liked California, and I enjoyed the work in the shipyard. I made many friends.

I often wonder about my co-workers. I worked side-by-side with a woman named Wassa, and I've always wondered what became of her.

My Mother

by Kate Weeks Grant
Moore, Oklahoma
about her mother, Clara Brown Weeks

Clara Brown Weeks

On September 3, 1899, my mother was born in Cheyenne, Oklahoma while her parents, George and Nancy Walters Brown, were traveling from New Mexico by covered wagon to Canadian, Oklahoma with their only child, Ethel, age two. They settled in Canadian, Oklahoma and reared nine children.

After my mother finished school, she desired to be a nurse. She worked as a telephone operator and met a tall, good-looking man with black hair and brown eyes, and he was also a fast talker. My mother was to leave to go to Chicago, Illinois for nurses training, but Bill Weeks (born September 4, 1897) persuaded her to get married the day before she was to leave. They married April 11, 1916 in Canadian.

My mother became a farmer's wife and reared seven

children to be grown and married. In her later years, she finished her nurses training.

During World War II, in 1944-45, she began working in Bella Vista, California, at the Shell Oil Company where my Dad also worked. My Mom and Dad were so strong for all of us grown children during the war, while our husbands were overseas or working on the home front. They helped with the grandchildren, especially my daughter Laquetta, and my sister's three sons, Leon, Ulas, and Eddie Kirby. Dad helped my sister and me often with repairs and driving us to the store. I don't know what we would have done without their strength when my sister Idell received the news that her husband had been killed in Okinawa.

Later my mother was able to continue her career as a nurse, and was employed as a nurse for 15 years before her death on April 16, 1967. What a wonderful mother, mother-in-law, grandmother, great-grandmother, and a very caring nurse. I miss her.

Bill and Clara Weeks

Riveting With the Marines
by Rosemary V. Clark Whitlock
Lancaster, South Carolina

Rosemary on her wedding day in 1944 (left) and on her 80th birthday in 2006. Note the "Rosie" cake that says, "Rosie rivets at 80!"

I was 16 years old in 1942 when I passed the course at the National Youth Administration Trade School. I informed the director that I had decided on the Quantico Marine Base at Quantico, Virginia. He seemed pleased and set in motion the process of application.

Living quarters in Fredericksburg was as near as he could place me to Quantico. Quantico is just about non-existent as a town. Quantico's fame lies in its Air Marine Corps Base. The base incorporates huge technological research and developmental grounds and base operations. The base owns many acres, some of which are for environmental preservation. The base's entrance, with its impressive monument of fighting Marines protecting America's borders, is only 20 miles from Fredericksburg on Route 1. It is only 36 miles from Washington, D.C.

The damaged planes were brought in, needing more than one type of repair from battles. They were brought in with radios malfunctioning. Panels of instruments had to be tested for repair. Paint was often threadbare. Engine parts were worn. Wing flaps and landing gear were sometimes unaligned. Wings were damaged, requiring replacement of metal in some areas and always needing new rivets and screws. In other words, the body, the guts, everything that makes up a whole airplane had to be gone over with a fine-toothed comb. Therefore, a mighty crowd of skilled Marines and their assistants from many and varied shop areas were present outside for an airplane's return to service.

There was always a moment of tense silence as the plane taxied onto the runway. Were we as skilled as we needed to be? Had any of us missed anything we were responsible for discovering and repairing? Then our imaginations really went wild. What if the plane could not fly?

The lift-off was always accompanied by our silent agony. Then, as the plane soared like an eagle, gaining height above the water, a shout of jubilation rose as the plane rose. Waving arms and leaping bodies bid it farewell. A plane was back in service. A pilot and his crew were back in the air, doing what they did best. Together, we were all helping win the war. What a gigantic thrill it was each time, to watch a Grumman F6F-3 Hellcat leave the ground and soar over the Potomac River and rise above the clouds! Elatedly, we returned to the hangers to resume work on yet another Hellcat.

I became a leader with an assistant, and I was moved to another wing. I was given a six cents raise, too. When a co-worker, Frank, and I finished our last day of working together, he grinned and said in farewell, "Congrats, Rosemary, I'll miss you, but you've earned your production wings."

"I couldn't have done it without your wisdom and expertise. Thank you, Captain Murphy."

Rosemary visited the U. S. Marine Air-Ground Museum at Quantico in 1989.

Wrong Versus Right Brother

by Rosemary V. Clark Whitlock
Lancaster, South Carolina

Left: Kenny and Rosemary leaving for Florida in a 1938 Ford convertible, going on a second honeymoon to celebrate Kenny's return from WW II in May 1946. Right: Kenny and Rosemary on a "trip down memory lane" at Quantico in July 1989.

My name is Rosemary Clark Whitlock. I came home to Covington, Virginia from Quantico Marine Air-Ground Base in Quantico, Virginia. I was a riveter, helping repair Grumman F6F-3 Hellcat fighter airplanes.

The year and month was January 1944. Kenneth Whitlock came home on a 7-day pass from an Army base where he was stationed in Georgia. I went on a date with Kenny's brother and met Kenny. It really was love at first sight with Kenny and me.

Kenny asked me for a date. There were only three days left of his pass. We spent the first of those three days sight-seeing around the county, taking pictures and talking of many things. The next day we spent at Natural Bridge, Lexington, Virginia. We talked about this war-torn world and what would the future hold for us, for America?

Kenny tried to carve our initials into the rocky wall of the bridge with just his pocket knife Then he said, "I've fallen in love with you and I hope you have with me. Will you marry me?" Within the circle of his arms the world melted away, and there was just he and I. I told Kenny that within this war-torn world, we should move slowly on matters of the heart.

The next night, seated in his car on Main Street after attending the movie, *The Song of Bernadette*, I told Kenny, "I've taken more time to think it over and yes I'll marry you."

Kenny yelled, "WOW!" Then he kissed me thoroughly. A policeman tapped on the car's window. Kenny rolled down the window and said, "Yes sir?"

The walking cop said, "Stop kissing on Main Street."

Kenny answered, "Sir, I'm leaving on the midnight train. We've just become engaged."

The policeman said, "Carry on, soldier."

Kenny shipped overseas in October and was shipwrecked on the way. A French corvette ship rescued all but 30 men. I didn't return to Quantico. I went to work at an Industrial Rayon Corporation plant in Covington, Virginia. We spun cones of rayon thread that was then woven into silk and satin materials for use in the war effort. The material was used mostly for linings of coffins during wartime.

Kenny and I married on another 3-day pass in May 1944. He came home from Germany in April 1946. It wasn't all roses with the world and us adjusting to peacetime, but we soon got the jigsaw pieces worked out, and life became our bowl of cherries. We raised four wonderful children. Kenny died on November 29, 1990. He lives on in my heart.

Oh, the one date I had with the wrong brother was only a friendly date. We both knew that, even before the date. No sparks flew between us. But when I met Kenny, the whole sky lit up with fireworks for both of us.

Rosemary with her four children in 2006

Rosie Works in Arsenal While Waiting For the Love of Her Life

by
Dorothy Wills-Raftery

about her mother,
Dorothy Gennewein Wills
Kingston, New York

Dorothy in her Watervliet Arsenal uniform in the 1940's

When World War II broke out, a wave of patriotism flooded our nation. Every man, woman, and child wanted to do something to help the war effort. It was a generation of heroes, both overseas and on the home front.

In 1941, my father, Staff Sergeant Earl "Larry" Wills, was a soldier in the U. S. Army's First Division (the "Big Red One"). My mother, Dorothy Gennewein Wills, lived at home with her parents in Ridgewood, New York. This was a time when there were no cell phones and no computers for Email, and postal mail was censored. My mother had to patiently wait and keep the faith that she would soon hear from the love of her life, either via postal mail, telegram, or a rare telephone call.

Since my grandparents did not have a telephone in their house, my mother used to frequent the nearby corner candy store, as it was one of the few places to have a telephone during those days. When my father wrote to my mother, he would indicate what day he would try to phone her and she would eagerly wait in that candy store for the call. On the days when his call would come through at a different time, the owners of the candy store would rush two doors down to my grandparents' apartment to notify Mom that my father was on the phone. She would race to that store as if carried by the wind to receive his call.

When my father and his unit were shipped overseas, my mother also wanted to do her part. Initially, she wanted to join the WACS (Women's Army Corps), but my father wanted her to remain stateside. Determined to participate, Mom moved from Ridgewood to the upstate Troy/Cohoes area, where she resided with her sister-in-law so she could work in the Watervliet Arsenal near Albany. There, Mom—a true Rosie the Riveter dressed in a uniform and hat, stationed under an assembly line where large cannons moved overhead—worked on a lathe making cannon reamers.

"We all wanted to help out," recalls my mother. "I was proud of my husband, I was proud of our country, and I was proud to work in the Watervliet Arsenal."

More than a year later, Mom moved back home at the request of her mother. One memorable day, there was a knock on my grandparents' door and when Mom answered, she was greeted by a delivery of 18 long-stemmed red symbolic roses. . . one rose marking each month my father served overseas.

"I knew when I received those roses that my husband was coming home," remembers my Mom. "That was one of the happiest days of my life." Needless to say, since that day, the red rose has always been my mother's favorite flower.

A Proud Rosie the Riveter

by
Mary Wingler

Sun City West,
Arizona

Mary, wearing her fur coat and standing in front of the house in which she stayed in Connersville, Indiana, 1943-44

I was just a sophomore in high school when I heard the frantic radio reporter detailing the Japanese attack on Pearl Harbor. It would be two years later, following my graduation from Hindsboro (Illinois) Community High School, that my opportunity to serve my country would arrive.

Even at the young age of 17, I knew I wanted to help the war effort. My father had been a World War I veteran, serving in the Navy, but had died when I was just 11 years old, leaving my mother to singly raise myself and my little brother. Mother received a military death benefit, which allowed her to attend beautician school to support our family.

Now that the next World War was on, Mother shared my patriotism and advised me to talk to another local young woman, "Toots" Ramsey Harvey, who had graduated a year ahead of me. Toots just happened to be home that week, visiting her parents. She was working in Connersville, Indiana as an inspector at the American Central Defense Plant. Toots was very positive about my being employed at the plant, and encouraged me to go back to Connersville with her and apply for a position.

I went home, packed my suitcase, and the next day we boarded the train for Indianapolis, Indiana. When we arrived, we were met by a bus that actually was a cattle trailer with bench seats along the sides. We had a 3-hour bumpy ride before Connersville came into view. In the summer, this open-air ride was stifling hot, while in the winter it was freezing cold!

We stayed at Toots' cousin's home. The next morning, we arrived early at the plant and I was hired immediately. My first training was in how to use a rivet gun. It was very important to hold the rivet straight, to ensure that it would hold the two sheets of metal together. This metal was the spar part of the wing on a B-17 bomber. I became very efficient and could rivet five spars in a day. The finished wings were then sent to Texas to be assembled onto the aircraft. It was important to me to do my job correctly, realizing the danger to a plane having faulty riveting.

I worked 10 hours a day, 6 days a week, with two 15-minute breaks and a half-hour lunch break. We prepared our own lunches and brought them in our little black buckets. My initial wages were 60 cents per hour, $39.69 per week. However, in just a couple of months our wages were raised to $1.00 per hour. I was in "hog heaven" with such a large paycheck.

My mother called one day and asked if I would like to buy a fur coat, as they had just received a few coats in the local dress store. She made the purchase and I sent money out of every paycheck to reimburse her generous act. We soon moved to a large two-story, red brick house. Five of us women working in the plant lived together, each paying our landlord $3.00 per week.

On July 22, 1944, the men and women of the American Central Manufacturing Corporation were presented the Army-Navy "E" Award for the plant's outstanding production of war equipment. A ceremony and picnic were held to honor all the employees. Each person in the plant received a lapel pin for distinguished service to our country, which I proudly wore. My mother traveled 150 miles to be in attendance. I know she was just as proud as I was to have contributed towards the war effort.

I returned to our home and later married my high school boyfriend, Lowell Wingler. We farmed more than 800 acres in central Illinois and raised two daughters—a special education teacher and a veterinarian.

My Mother's Story

by Mary Womack
Okeana, Ohio
about her mother,
Mary Magdalene "Maggie" Forth Womack

Maggie Womack

This story captures an important aspect of a time that can never be forgotten. It was a war. It was a struggle for survival not only on the war front, but also on the home front. World War II changed us forever, and put women in the workplace forever.

My mother, Mary Magdalene Forth Womack, known as Maggie, was born in 1900. At the age of 42, she went to work at the Viola Naval Ordnance Plant, a wartime shell-loading factory in Viola, Kentucky.

Maggie and her close-knit family lived in Mayfield, Kentucky. She was married to Nover Womack, who was reporting for duty when the President said that men over 40 would not be drafted. Consequently, he went to work in the Viola factory. Maggie was the mother of three: William Womack, who served in England during the war when the Germans were bombing; Leola Marie Womack Brown, who worked in the Viola factory, and I was a baby at the time. Maggie also raised her nephew Harold, whose mother died during childbirth. She helped with her infant grandson when her daughter-in-law worked at Viola.

Maggie was a generous, compassionate person. She always gave food and water to strangers who arrived at her doorstep, even though many foods, such as sugar, coffee, and shortening, were in short supply.

Prior to the war, Maggie worked at Merit Clothing Mills, making men's suits, and then uniforms when the war started. Maggie then worked at the Graves County Viola plant from 1942-1945. The plant paid the best wages at the time - $1.00 an hour. Built on an open field surrounded by a fence with armed guards, an identification card had to be presented to gain entrance. Since gas was rationed, Maggie rode the bus, paying $1.00 in bus fare each day.

Maggie worked 8-hour shifts, sitting in a small room at a rectangular table with about 25 women, who performed various steps in making ammunition. Maggie worked on "The Fuse," putting pellets, referred to as tetrol, into small vial-like containers. She wore a canvas apron, but no protective clothing, no head covering, and no gloves. She handled yellow pellets, and they penetrated the skin. Powder from pellets flaked off and was breathed when performing this task. Maggie's hair turned yellow. Her hands, arms, and finally her face turned yellow. My mother continued to work as though nothing was unusual, and when she stopped working, her skin color returned to normal. Her yellow hair grew out over time.

At the war's end, this ammunition factory was dismantled without a trace of its existence.

Where Blue Columbines Grow

by Barbara J. Sothman Worthey
Sun City West, Arizona

Barbara and Joe in 1942 (left)
and on their 60th wedding anniversary

December 7, 1941, the sneak attack on Pearl Harbor. Joe and I were high school sweethearts in Greeley, Colorado. We danced in the gym during noon socials, snow skied on weekends, and shared a Coke with hamburgers and chips at Jessie's Drive-in.

Several months after Pearl, Joe said, "Let's drive to Estes Park and enjoy the moonlight." Snow-capped mountains bathed in moonlight, fresh pine-scented breezes . . . yeah! As we drove up the Big Thompson Canyon, we listened to the Lucky Strike Hit Parade. We sang along with "Yours": *"Yours till the end of life's story . . ."*

It became "our" song.

Somewhere between Estes Park and Glen Haven, we parked the car. The bright moon cast a long silver path across a field concealed with the last snow of winter.

"Soon the mountains and meadows will be a blanket of Blue Columbines," I said wistfully.

"Yeah, but now we are stuck!" replied Joe. He rocked the car back and forth. It remained unmovable.

"We... are... stuck."

"No kidding," I smiled suspiciously.

With a glint in his eye, he held out his hand and said, "Either say 'yes' and take this ring, or get out and push!"

Joe is a great romantic!

He pushed as I drove the car, thrilled with my sparkling engagement ring. We were married in the Presbyterian Church in La Salle, Colorado.

With $60 and "stars in our eyes," we went to southern California. This is where my Rosie the Riveter career began. I worked on lathes, milling machines, and drill presses in several war plants before we returned to Colorado where Joe enlisted in the Army Air Force. We parted ways but I was determined to follow him whenever and however I could. I began working for United Air Lines in Cheyenne, Wyoming, cleaning and testing spark plugs for military aircraft. From Greeley, I traveled by bus 100 miles round trip each day. Every night, I wrote a letter to my Joe.

Then I went to Lynchburg, Virginia, where I sewed stacks of green G.I. socks. On to St. Louis, Missouri, where I worked for Boeing Aircraft. I riveted and bucked rivets on the huge wings of B-29 and B-17 bombers. With the birth of our son Mike, my "Rosie" career ended.

Every spring in our beautiful Colorado mountains, nature will perform her incredible magic. The winter's snow will slowly melt, then blankets of alpine flowers will awaken from their long sleep and burst into colorful bloom. It has been 64 wonderful years since that enchanting moonlit winter night, and we are still counting.

High in the mountains, where Blue Columbines grow,
Between Estes Park, and Glen Haven please go.
Gently lay our ashes, upon the soft white snow,
Our love will continue, where Blue Columbines grow.

Forever each spring, after the melting of snow,
Lovers will thrill, with the mountains aglow.
On the steep hillsides, the green meadows will show,
Our love is eternal, where Blue Columbines grow.

- Barbara J. Sothman Worthey

Memories of World War 2
by M. Hope Midkiff Wright
Elizabethtown, Kentucky

Pvt. Hope Wright (on the right) with her friend, Pvt. Rosella Jones, in November 1944 on their first furlough after joining the WACS (Women's Air Corps). Before joining the WACS, Hope worked as a Rosie in a sheet metal shop.

    I was a senior at Pax (West Virginia) High School when the war started. I quit school, much to my parents' disappointment, and went to South Charleston, West Virginia, for training through the NYA to be a welder. I lived in St. Albans, West Virginia, where I met my best friend for life, Rosella Jones. We went to Patterson Field, Ohio, where we worked in the sheet metal shop.

    My fondest memories are the nice, interesting people we worked with, plus our landlady, Fern Frame. We lived in Springfield, Ohio. She treated us like kin, bringing us hot cocoa and cookies on Sunday mornings.

    I remember them all – Mr. Bush, who was surprised that we could work with blueprints. Pappy Reeves, who kept in touch with four of us girls (Vivian, June, Rosella, and me) for the rest of his life. Rosie Rosenbloom, who brought us candy. Victor Spitznagle, who had a car, took us to Cincinnati swimming, and to Coney Island. His letters stopped suddenly after he left England. I still have pictures and a lapel pin he sent me from London. Then there was Willard Barnett, who took us to work every day. Later, he and Vivian married.

After two years, Rosella and I decided to join the WACS (Women's Army Corps). We took basic training at Fort Des Moines, Iowa in July 1944. It rained all the time. I can still smell those long raincoats that had been stored in moth balls. We went to Moses Lake, Washington, attached to the 4th Army Air Corps for six months. I worked in the tool crib, she in the hangar next door. Then she went to March Field in California, and I went to Geiger Field near Spokane, Washington, as a stock records clerk.

In June 1945, my high school sweetheart, Brace (we met when I was 13 and he was 15), who had been a Prisoner of War in Germany, was released, and he called me from Staten Island. He asked me to marry him. I got a furlough and we were married June 21 in Weirwood, West Virginia, at my parents' home. After two weeks, he went to Florida and I went back to Washington. I was discharged on December 21, 1945. After five days and four nights, day coach, on the Great Northern Railroad, I finally saw him again on December 26, 1945. I went back to school and graduated from Pax High School on May 21, 1946 with my 16-year-old sister, Joanne, and my sister-in-law, Bernice.

Brace and Hope Wright in June 1997

Brace died on New Year's Day 2002, after 47½ years of marriage, during which time we had three sons, Wilfred, James (deceased), and Duane.

GOD BLESS AMERICA FOREVER.

Rosie – The Airplane Mechanic

by Elaine Gehri Lambers Young
Seattle, Washington

Elaine Young at her workbench

In 1941, I was 15 years old when the Second World War broke out. A call went out, asking for women to come and help build airplanes. So, my mother and I went to Sand Point Naval Air Station in Seattle, Washington to sign up. I told them I was 17 years old, since I always looked older than my age. I was accepted, but my mother was not. They told her she had diabetes and was she ever shocked!

I started out as a Mechanics' Helper. They sent me to Edison Vocational School to learn tools and how to use them. I was there for six months. I worked on the nose section of the PBY's, which had two Pratt and Whitney (Twin Wasp radial piston) engines in them. These planes did the bombing in Japan and were

PBY4
www.history101.com

highly vulnerable to anti-aircraft attacks.

Matter of fact, during my time at the Naval Air Station, there were two PBY's that fell into Lake Washington and are still there to this day. There have been television programs that have done stories on these planes and have shown underwater pictures of them lying at the bottom of the lake.

I was at the Naval Air Station for five years, and during that time I met my future husband, Sidney Lambers. He was the Chief Petty Officer on my floor at the A & R Hangar. However, whenever our breaks came around, I was always surrounded by sailors and my future husband never had a chance to interrupt! But guess who I married in 1945?

When the boys started coming home, I gave up my job so they could have a job. On some of my evenings after work, I would go to the NSO's and serve the boys refreshments and also would dance with them. I felt it was an honor to be of service to the good ole USA!

Today I am so grateful to have had this job and be sent to school to learn the tools. To this day, it has helped me immensely in taking care of my home. I have been in my home for 50 years. I have a large tool and work bench, which I use at least once a day. I also do a lot of craft projects, and the work bench has come in quite handy.

In addition, since 1991 the backyard of my home has been listed as a Backyard Wildlife Sanctuary. I thoroughly enjoy all the various wildlife I feed and talk to every day.

Elaine's yard is a Wildlife Sanctuary.

Index

of names, places of work, and types of work

A

A-20 airplane, 198
A. O. Smith, 169
Aero Parts (Boeing), 53
Air raid, 36, 126, 178
Airplane production (other than riveting), 13, 16, 26, 30, 33, 34, 40, 51, 57, 69, 75, 79, 80, 83, 85, 86, 87, 106, 112, 120, 126, 130, 136, 137, 147, 151, 153, 168, 182, 192, 193, 195
Allen, Jane E., 1
Allen, Maggie, 1
American Central Defense Plant, 187
American Rolbal, 26
Ammunition production, 11, 23, 24, 46, 79, 94, 119, 147, 186, 189, 190
Ankeny Ordnance Plant, 119
Anthoine, Elizabeth Parker, 3
Arkansas Ordnance Plant, 11
Armour, Anna Lee, 5
Arundale, Hazel, 7
Asseo, Sam, 145, 146
Atomic bomb, 16, 44, 69, 72, 102, 138

B

B-17 airplane, 8, 51, 62, 81, 93, 100, 115, 116, 120, 133, 188, 192
B-24 airplane, 4, 52, 62, 84, 106
B-25 airplane, 130, 168
B-26 airplane, 137
B-27 airplane, 13

B-29 airplane, 79, 108, 168, 192
Baker, Norma Jean, 7
Barney, Julia June, 9
Baskin, Minnie Furn, 11
Beck, Genevieve E., 13
Beck, Sammy Laughlin, 15
Beckham, Helen Barney, 9
Beech Aircraft, 5
Bell Bomber Plant, 57, 108
Bechtel McComb Parsons aircraft modification plant, 27
Blackouts, 4, 170
Blume, Odean Gregg, 17, 19
Boeing Aircraft Company, 5, 9, 10, 53, 69, 93, 133, 173, 192
Border defense, 14, 35, 59, 60, 178
Bowerman, Ruby Lee Eversole, 21
Boyes, Ginevra, 67
Brewster Aircraft, 151
Briggs and Stratton Airplane Company, 86
Briggs Manufacturing, 115
Brockmann, Donna, 130
Brown, Leola Marie Womack, 23
Brown, Normalie, 53, 54
Brummett, Laquetta Grant, 65
Bruno, Julia Regina, 25
Bucking rivets, 3, 14, 16, 44, 52, 120, 124, 134, 192
Burgess-Cook, Paula, 161

C

C-47 airplane, 16, 52, 55, 56, 75,

199

76, 112, 124, 144, 145, 146, 162
Camp Anza, 156
Camp Breckenridge, 86
Camp Butner, 6
Camp Cook, 69
Camp Parks, 141
Camp Shelby, 27, 28, 45
Camp Wheeler, 101
Cargill, Thorval, 47
Carter, Frances Tunnell, 27, 29
Carter, John T., 27, 29
Cessna, 5
Clasen, Darcy, 31
Clasen, Douglas Michael, 31
Clasen, Jonnie Melillo, 31, 39, 83, 91, 101, 125, 167
Clasen, Laura Belle Seim, 31
Clerk, 10, 77, 106, 129, 130
Cole, Shirley Marie Jackson, 33, 35
Coleman, Rena, 165
Consolidated Vultee Aircraft, 33, 105, 106
Convair Aircraft, 99, 119
Cornhusker Bomb Plant, 93
Coulombe, Rochelle, 59
Curtiss-Wright Airplane Plant, 141

DC-3 airplane, 104
Denver Modification Center, 8
Denyer, Alyson Miller, 103
Doak Aircraft Company, 147
Domenick, Mary Lou FitzGerald, 37
Douglas Aircraft (California), 7, 81, 87, 112, 113

Douglas Aircraft (Oklahoma), 16, 55, 75, 124, 143, 145, 162

Draftsman, 37, 57, 58, 137
Drill press operator, 16

Edwards, Dorothy Garzik, 39
Edwards, Paul, 39
Edwards, Viola Gertrude Rector, 41
Enterprise Aluminum Company, 91

F

F6F-3 Hellcat airplane, 182, 183
Fairbanks Morse, 98
Farming, 1, 2, 117, 134
Feige, Josephine C. Farruggio, 43
Fiala, Margaret Such, 45
Fields, Thoral Juanita Cargill, 47, 49
Firestone Park, 103
Fisher Body Aircraft, 149
Fisher, Elizabeth, 51
Flowers, Wanda Duffy, 53
Ford, Bacon, and Davis, 11
Forrester, Ava Walton, 55
Fort Benning, 6
Fort Bliss, 18
Fort Bragg, 104
Fort Brown, 17
Fort Custer, 155
Fort Des Moines, 194
Fort Lewis, 62
Fort Stewart, 172
Frankel, Harriet R., 57

Gano, Ruby, 59
Gareis, Dolores, 43
Gedney, Lois Reynolds, 61
Geiger Field, 194

Glenn L. Martin Company, 43, 137
Goodyear, 11
Gowan Field, 52, 72
Graham, Jean, 83
Grant, Kate Weeks, 63, 65, 67, 179
Grumman Aircraft, 40

H

Hamilton, Dorine Smith, 69
Harrison, Gar-Fay, 71
Harvey, "Toots" Ramsey, 187
Hawkins, Anniece Aikins, 73
Heck, Zola Walton, 75
Hellcat airplane, 40, 182, 183
Hicks, Karen, 147
Holloway, Jean M., 77
Horton, Michael, 79
Horton, Ruth Hutchens, 79
Hunter Field, 160, 172

I

Industrial Rayon Corporation, 184
Inspector, 8, 41, 84, 95, 187

J

Jackson, Clara Louise Owens, 35
Jayme, Gladys Marley Eckels, 81
Jaynes, Joyce, 177
Johnson, Jean Graham, 83
Jones, Rosella, 193

K

Kaiser Shipyards, 47, 61, 63, 65, 68, 163, 164, 174, 177

Kellogg, 155
Kenrad Corporation, 85, 86
Kidd, Willie Lou Moore Mitchell, 85
Kizer, Amelia Mathauser, 133, 134
Klotz, Nancy Treu, 169

L

Lake City Ammunition, 41
Lazerus, Lorraine Koop, 87
Lewis, Dorothy "Lucy" Case, 89
Liberty Ships, 48, 160, 175
Linch, Thelma Aides Fuller, 91, 101
Lockheed, 21, 58

M

March Field, 194
Mare Island, 174
Martin, Lucy Mae, 53, 54
Mathauser, Emma, 93
Mayernick, Helen, 95
McCray, Elaine G. Manthey, 97
McMillan, Eloise Snow, 99
Melillo, Frankie Doris Thompson, 91
Merit Clothing Mills, 190
Military assistance, 19, 101, 109, 128,
Miller, Dorothy Margaret Smith, 103
Minchew, Kenley, 99, 121
Mollberg, Maebeth, 105
Monroe, Marilyn, 7
Moss, Jessie Belle, 107
Mountain Home Army Air Field, 72
Myrick, Mabel W., 109

N

National Women's History Museum, 138
Nelsen, Margaret Neuhauer, 111
Nelson, Opal Land, 113
Nickell, Opal Breeding, 115
North American Aircraft, 41

O

Oregon Shipyards, 175
Orlando Air Base, 13

P

P–38 airplane, 22
PBY airplanes, 195
Packard Aircraft, 95
Parachute production, 90
Parks, Hazel Young, 117
Patterson Air Field, 168, 193
Pearce, June Olander, 99, 119, 121
Pearl Harbor, 7, 15, 20, 21, 22, 25, 29, 35, 43, 55, 59, 73, 75, 81, 97, 99, 105, 119, 129, 147, 163, 187, 191
Pedder, Donna Clasen, 31
Penner, Nona Vanita McLemore, 123
Pentagon worker, 109
Peters, Carol, 73
Pettit, Carlotta de la Cruz, 125
Picatinny Arsenal, 40
Plane-spotting, 59, 139

Pope, Verlie Roberts, 127
Port Chicago Naval Magazine, 164
Powell, Kathleen O., 129
Pratt-Whitney Defense Plant, 41
Price, Delores, 131
Prindle, Linda, 149

Pullman Aircraft, 52

Q

Quantico Marine Base, 181, 183

R

Ration stamps, 15, 44, 123, 164, 166, 170, 190
Red Cross, 42, 78, 98, 106, 123
Rees, Wilma Mathauser, 93, 133, 134
Rinta, Violet, 137
Riveting, 3, 5, 7, 12, 14, 16, 22, 27, 40, 44, 52, 53, 54, 55, 80, 81, 84, 100, 103, 104, 108, 113, 115, 120, 124, 145, 150, 157, 162, 168, 173, 181, 182, 183, 188, 192
Robins Field, 3
Romans, Hazel, 101
Roner, Donna Ruth Shrauger, 135
Rosie the Riveter World War II/Home Front National Historical Park, 172
Rowe, Drusilla Durham Methvin, 72, 137

S

Sand Point Naval Air Station, 195
Savanna Army Depot, 147
Scrap metal (saving), 15, 53, 136, 163
Scudder, Erma Ellis, 139
Scudder, Kandis L., 139
Seattle Port of Embarkation, 88
Sedwick, Ruth Slack, 141
Semrad, Darlene Crozier, 143, 145
Sewell, Emma Mummert, 147

Shell Oil Company, 180
Shipyard worker (other than welding), 26, 47, 48, 49, 61, 71, 174
Shuits, Clara Laughlin, 15
Siemens, Edna Agnes Jackson, 149
Smith, Dorothy Edwards, 39
Smith, Romaine Stone, 151
Southeastern Shipyard, 159, 172
Spahn, Emily Rice, 153
Spartan Aeronautics, 79
Spriggs, Laura B., 155
Sunflower Powder, 41
Swallow Aircraft Company, 5

T

Tank production, 44
Tasset, Clarentine Blasi, 157
Taylor, Betty Tucker, 159
Taylor, Ruby Hutchens, 79
Tent production, 42, 131
Thiessen, Alma, 54
Thiessen, Dorothy, 54
Thomas, Carrie Hill, 161
Thompson, Allie Mae, 163, 165
Tibbitts, Frances, 61
Tinker Field, 55, 75, 79, 143, 145
Tinker, June Midkiff, 167
Treu, Bertha T., 169
Troop train, 11, 21, 28, 120, 171, 177
Tucker, Lucretia Jane, 171

U

United Airlines, 51, 192
USO, 14, 27, 34, 71, 84, 196

V

Van Alstine, Marjorie Backlin, 173

Vance Air Force Base, 143
Victory garden, 1, 2, 15, 32, 44, 123, 164
Victory Ships, 48
Viola Naval Ordnance Plant, 23, 189
Vultee Aircraft, 33, 105, 106

W

WACS, 186, 193, 194
Waldroff, Nelle Eatherton, 175
Walker, Lillian Beatrice Sanderson, 177
Walton, Zona, 75
War bonds, 71, 74, 172
Watervliet Arsenal, 185, 186
Watson Flagg Machine Company, 77
WAVES, 21, 57
Weeks, Clara Brown, 179
Welding, 26, 156, 64, 65, 68, 159, 163, 165, 168, 172, 175, 177, 193, 197
Western Union, 127
Whitlock, Rosemary V. Clark, 181, 183
Willow Run Bomber Plant, 84
Wills-Raftery, Dorothy, 185
Wilmington Shipyards, 156
Wingler, Mary, 187
Womack, Mary, 189
Womack, Mary Magdalene Forth, 189
Worthy, Barbara Sothman, 191
Wright, Hope Midkiff, 168, 193

X-Y-Z

Young, Elaine Gehri Lambers, 195

American Rosie the Riveter Association®

PURPOSES:

To recognize and preserve the history and legacy of working women, including volunteer women, during World War II; to promote cooperation and fellowship among such members and their descendants; to encourage excellence and responsibility in all types of work without regard to gender, and to promote the advancement of patriotic ideals and loyalty to the United States of America.

WHO MAY BELONG?

Women whose work during 1941-1945 was designed to contribute to the war effort (including women who did volunteer work) and their female descendants are eligible for active membership. Spouses and male relatives may become auxiliary members by attending an official local or national meeting of the Association.

Women who performed the work are known as **Rosies**. Their female descendants are **Rosebuds**. Male auxiliary members are known as **Rivets**. Qualifying work for Rosies may consist of:

1. Employment of any sort in an industry or government agency directly related to the war effort, **or**

2. Employment, including self-employment (such as farming), in a capacity usually held by a man, thus releasing the man for military duty, **or**

3. Participation on a sustained basis in one or more volunteer activities related to the war effort.

Rosebuds and **Rivets** are eligible for membership, regardless of whether their Rosie is living or deceased, and whether or not the Rosie was a member of the Association. Membership applications may be obtained at www.rosietheriveter.net or by contacting Executive Director Fran Carter, 209 University Park Drive, Birmingham, Alabama 35209, (205) 822-4106, fran.carter@juno.com.

Enjoy all of these historical books published by the American Rosie the Riveter Association®:

103 Rosie the Riveter Stories (2001)

Rosie the Riveter Celebration Cookbook (2004)

104 More Rosie the Riveter Stories (2005)

Rosie Romances and Other Rosie the Riveter Stories (2008)

Copies of all of these books may be ordered from:
    ARRA Books
    P.O. Box 188
    Kimberly, AL 35091

Hear the stories from the Rosies themselves!